ELEVATE YOUR MIND TO SUCCESS

Take Your Thoughts to a Higher Level

Jill Fandrich, PharmD

ISBN 979-8-88851-099-5 (Paperback)
ISBN 979-8-88851-101-5 (Hardcover)
ISBN 979-8-88851-100-8 (Digital)

Covenant Books
11661 Hwy 707
Murrells Inlet, SC 29576
www.covenantbooks.com

CONTENTS

INTRODUCTION FOR *ELEVATE YOUR MIND TO SUCCESS*

Have you ever wondered why success seems to come more easily for some people than others? Where are you along your journey? Do negative or unsupportive thoughts ever prevent you from climbing higher? What if you could exchange your negative thoughts for positive and favorable ones and "elevate" yourself to a higher level of thinking? What if you could "elevate" your mind to *successful* thinking?

Whatever you dwell on most gets the majority of your energy and action. This book will give you the tools and insight needed to alter and greatly improve the "programming" of your thoughts, causing you to focus on successful thinking. This will improve your ability to lead with confidence and candor while increasing your ability to handle any situation. Success means different things to different people. It all starts with the thoughts that you think. How much effort will you put into programming your mind with a winning foundation?

A lack of "proper" thinking appears to have crept into our society. I have personally experienced this negative, harmful thinking and have witnessed it in other people and even companies, which has shown me the need to bring forth a book such as this. What if you could alter the way you think and the thoughts you dwell upon, even to the point that positive thinking becomes a predictable inclination? What if your responses become more favorable and supportive of your current circumstances? What would it take for you to develop this type of thinking to the point that it becomes an automatic "habit"?

I have come to realize the need to return to the basics of leadership training. Before considering how other people affect us and our responses, we must first take responsibility for ourselves and how we "react" to any given situation. We cannot control other people and what they choose to do. But we can control ourselves and how we respond. And we must look to the source of our responses, which is how we have allowed ourselves to think. Once we take responsibility for our own thought processes, we can then recognize that there is also a need to develop the finesse, compassion, and especially the fine art of getting along with other people in everyday interactions.

In preparation for writing this book, I studied people, books, behaviors, and both negative and positive thoughts and reactions. I discussed peoples' thoughts and why they responded the way they did. I read numerous resources regarding each subject and human behavior. I observed charismatic professionals and not-so-eloquent ones as well! With each response, I visualized situations of relevance and how the responses could be applied to professional and personal settings. I also extrapolated key findings from my experience from both my professional career and personal encounters and organized the information in such a way that will be applicable from numerous perspectives. When applied, these principles, ideas, and strategies will prove to be effective, insightful, and *mind-altering*.

Relationships are the most important things in our lives. It is imperative that we reach an understanding of our own thoughts and how they affect nearly every aspect of our lives, as they ultimately affect others as well. Proverbs 23:7 (NKJV) describes this clearly as it reads, *"For as he thinks in his heart, so is he."* And also, *"Be careful what you think, because your thoughts run your life,"* Proverbs 4:23 (NCV). No pressure there! Knowing the importance of our thoughts, it is logical to focus a significant amount of time and energy on understanding the nature of them and how we can gain better control of them as well. And we recognize this is not a matter of our own "self-reliance," but rather, the true source comes only through the strength, guidance, and provisions of God our Creator.

This book is *indirectly* broken down into three parts. In the first part, we focus on awareness of our thoughts and *recognize* where they currently are. We also become "mindfully aware" of the energy involved with different thoughts, especially the difference between negative and positive thinking. Read or listen to this section with intention and determination while underlining, highlighting, or jotting down key points you want to either remove from your current programming or use to improve upon your current "configuration." While it may not be applicable to reframe every thought, read, reread, and relisten to each section in an attempt to reprogram the information into your mind so you are able to access these "files" when the opportunity presents itself. Return and refer to this section often, and even visualize the suggestions playing out in your own setting. Think about it often, and imagine different outcomes based on different programming each time.

Ask yourself:
"How might my thoughts be holding me back from the success I desire?"
"What changes do I need to make?"
"Where should I begin?"
"What part of my programming is already supportive?"
"What have I learned from this awareness?"

Journal your results and whether they are "in progress" or are already successes. Be sure to enter the dates of each entry and be specific regarding your process, how you responded, and what you did or did not like about your analysis. Review your journal weekly, or at least monthly, to monitor your progress and reveal how you are growing in the process.

In part two, we discuss recognizing and overcoming obstacles along the way. As with any undertaking you commit yourself to, there will always be challenges to overcome. Suggestions, ideas, and strategies are presented in order to "imprint" successful traits into your mind's programming and how to overcome or even prevent future concerns. While this is an enormous undertaking, learning about and truly understanding each of these obstacles will undoubtedly grow you as a person, provide a way for future prevention, and launch you as a refined leader.

Finally, part three involves conditioning, reframing, and reprogramming your newly decluttered mind. We will determine your specific personality type and discuss dozens of pertinent leadership skills necessary for growth and development. We seek to fill your mind with successful, encouraging, and inspiring traits and even habits, as we begin to understand what each of these skills looks like, as well as the characteristics and benefits of them. You will be enlightened, refreshed, energized, and empowered in your pursuit of a new approach and successful endeavor. Each chapter will conclude with wisdom, prayer, meditation, and reflection points, engaging you in thought-provoking interpretations.

Take time to answer each reflection request, and think about why you chose to answer the way you did. Perhaps focus on one chapter per week. Read or listen to each one slowly and highlight, underline, or jot down key points. As before, repeat the series of questions mentioned previously, and journal regarding your discoveries and progress. Be specific and include dates and times and specific notes of interest. Take time to identify who you know already that has and exemplifies the qualities or skills presented and what they look like. Then, decipher how you will incorporate them into both your professional and personal life. You will begin to notice them being displayed more and more naturally in all of your interactions. After the last skill has been processed, go back to the beginning!

These methods will allow you to get the most out of this book. Whether in a leadership position in the professional sector, a blue-collar employee, a church group class, head of your household, as a student online, or in a homeschooling setting, this book will masterfully remind you of the need to be deliberate about your thoughts, reframe them and replace if necessary, and display the love, kindness, respect, and compassion that should be built into the very nature of our being.

The time for action is *now*!

CHAPTER 1

Who Programmed My Mind?

I have come to the realization that my mind has been programmed by thousands of people who are not me! This reality has made me think and evaluate where I am in life and how this past programming has affected the events of my life up to this point. Is this where I would have chosen to be with different programming? Is this where I want to be now? How did I get here? Would I have been complacent here had I not figured this out?

I was instantly inspired by these thoughts and, I must admit, frustrated that I had allowed my mind, programmed by hundreds of other people, to control me for the majority of my life. It was a light bulb moment, which led to a fire-under-my-feet follow-up. I have not stopped moving since this discovery.

Have you ever stopped to think about the origins of your mind and thoughts? When did you realize they are mainly programmed by sources other than yourself? How does this make you feel? Do you think your life has been impacted by the preprogramming of your mind by others? No matter how hard you try, the contents you observe with your senses are generally derived from the information shared by other people. With the magnitude of technology today, multiple sources are often being used simultaneously—smartwatches, smartphones, smart TVs, smart-this, and smart-that. Everything has gotten so…smart! Or has it? All of these devices are constantly feeding you someone else's information—their viewpoint, their way of thinking, and even how they respond to situations or things.

Your mind is an accumulation of thoughts harvested since the day you were born. You have observed and absorbed memories, words, sounds, experiences, etc., from your very beginnings, and all of this information is filed in compartments in your brain. This data input first began from your parents or guardians, other family members, friends, teachers, news, media, and so on. Even as you educate yourself, you are still filling your mind with information someone else is telling you, as you have not personally experienced it nor witnessed the events yourself. Most of what you learn is from the instruction, words, or experience of someone else.

All of this information forms thoughts in your mind, which leads to how you feel. When situations or events happen to you each day, you respond to them based on how you feel from your mind, which has been programmed through your history of absorption of information and experiences. So, essentially, when you respond to an event, your mind already knows how it is going to react, and you do not even have to think about it. Therefore, the action you took was already preprogrammed.

Have you ever driven your car out of the driveway, and the next thing you realized was that you were already at your destination? You vaguely recall any of the journey. This is the astounding ability of your complex mind. Knowing this, does it not make sense to intentionally focus an abundance of time on the reprogramming of your mind? This bears repeating. Suppose your mind is already preprogrammed, and the way you respond or react in any given situation is determined in advance based on the programming of your mind. Isn't it imperative that you choose to focus a deliberate amount of time on your mind and essentially *retrain* your mind with a new program that aligns with how you "want" it to respond? In other words, with information that will allow it to instinctively respond in the way that *you* think is favorable and productive? Isn't it exciting to know you have the power to train your mind to provide supportive, empowering, and successful responses?

What is a thought?

So, what actually is a thought? Google says a thought is *"an idea or opinion produced by thinking, or occurring suddenly in the mind."* That is a little ambiguous, so let's find out more. *Merriam-Webster* defines *think* in a similarly indistinct way as *"to form or have in the mind."* According to Psychology Today, *"A thought is a representation of something. A representation is a likeness—a thing that depicts another thing by having characteristics that correspond to that other thing. For example, a picture, image, or mold of an object is a representation of that object."* And finally, *"thoughts are mental cognitions—our ideas, opinions, and beliefs about ourselves and the world around us."*[1]

While thoughts are generated based on information you take in from a variety of sources, thoughts are generally under your conscious control if you so choose. Essentially, if you allow yourself to become aware of your thoughts, you may elect to control, alter, and further direct them.

It is actually biblical to "capture" thoughts and control them. Second Corinthians 10:5 NIV reads, *"We take captive every thought to make it obedient to Christ."* This verse alone instructs you that you have the ability to isolate each thought you have and direct it as to how you want it to respond. *"Your minds may somehow be led astray from your sincere and pure devotion to Christ"* (2 Corinthians 11:3 NIV). You are taught that if there is anything out of sync with your thoughts, you must bring it to your awareness, make it obedient, and bring it under control. Expose your thoughts for what they are and to whom they are obedient, and deliberately bring them under control.

Now that a thought has been defined and exposed for what it really is, it is time to turn them into attainable, specific, and measurable goals. After becoming energized instantly upon all of these astounding "thought" discoveries, I decided to analyze my current situation and realized I had been aligned with a goal of being "comfortable." Not directly, per se, but I never really considered my true potential. I was conforming to the expectations of others without actually realizing it. Well, being comfortable is "nice," yet it made sense to me that rather than having this as a *goal*, it would naturally be a *by-product* of the more rewarding goal of being *successful, highly successful,* and in abundance.

When I write about success at any point throughout this book, I refer to success in any and all realms—business, personal life, spiritual life, financially, emotionally, in serving others, etc. It made logical sense for me to "upgrade" my goal from being simply comfortable to being wildly successful, and it started by reprogramming my mind and learning how successful people think. We will dive deeper into this topic in a future chapter.

This new insight led me down a reality path that I had never faced in my life before. I had spent most of my adult career practicing in a field that was not even my idea. I became well-educated in this field and dedicated myself to years of hard work, loyalty, and compassion, yet it was based on the "suggestion" of someone else! Only recently were my eyes opened to the fact that this was not my passion, my thoughts, or my true desire. I am extremely grateful for having had this opportunity and rewarding career. However, I am even more grateful to be able to identify my own thoughts and passions and am free to choose a new career I find so enjoyable that I cannot even call it work.

When you search your heart and mind, add to this your passion and desires, and what transpires is the love of something that comes easily to you and is joy-filled. What pops into your mind when you focus your thoughts on a passion? Is it what you are already doing? If so, you are amazing! You already figured out and acted upon your passions. If not, you are blessed to have an opportunity of discovery that awaits!

Belief system

God created your mind to be filled with peace, hope, and love. These all line up with your belief system. A belief is something you accept as true. And *"a belief system is an ideology or set of principles that help us to interpret our everyday reality."*[2] It is the way you view the world and is not necessarily correct or accurate. There are many different factors that influence the development of your belief system, including your upbringing, surrounding environment, knowledge sources, etc. Your belief system will determine how you make decisions and the type of decisions you make, as they are your perception of the way things are and what you believe to be true.

> *Beliefs are thoughts at rest.*
> —Larry Harvey

When you believe something to be true, rarely will you question or even think about the validity of it. It is often hard to reason logically with those who hold strong feelings about their beliefs rather than evidence-based logic. Beliefs are created both consciously and subconsciously. They are a map of your inner world and your outer world.

> *For as he thinks in his heart, so is he.*
> —Proverbs 23:7 NKJV

Fortunately, a belief system is changeable. It is important to challenge and update your beliefs often to ensure they are aligned with your values and support you in the way you want to go. You can change any desired behavior, thought pattern, or emotional state you wish. The first step to making changes is *awareness* of your preprogramming.

> *And you shall know the truth, and*
> *the truth shall make you free.*
> —John 8:32 NKJV

The following is a list of questions to ask yourself regarding your beliefs to reexamine limiting or negative ones:[3]

1. Where does this belief come from?
2. Is this my belief, or have I adopted it from someone else?
3. How does this belief help me?
4. How does this belief hinder me?

5.   How do I know this belief is true?
6.   What is my new and updated belief?

Core values

It is imperative that you clearly identify your core values. Without them, you are like a ship without a rudder. Rather than being able to choose a direction that aligns with your goals, you are at the mercy of the current. Identifying your beliefs and values ultimately helps you determine how you will operate your day-to-day life and how you will respond to your situations and surroundings. *"In order to make informed, aligned decisions and access how you actually feel about everything from your career to your friendships to your partnerships or to potential partnerships, you need to first figure out what really, truly matters to you. You need to figure out your values."*[4]

Simply put, if you have an indication of what your personal or professional values really are, you will be more likely to enter into situations where you are aligned with your beliefs and your goals. And when you are not, you will know something is off, and you will be able to use your beliefs and values as a guide to adjust to the situation, using your "internal compass."

Once you have identified your core values, you will be able to improve your life in abundant ways. Below are a few possible positive outcomes that may result from this alignment:

- Increased job satisfaction
- Improved performance
- Increased passion
- Greater joy, fulfillment, and contentment
- Greater authenticity and clarity about you
- Clearer boundaries
- Simplified decision-making
- Greater peace
- Improved confidence
- Increased overall happiness

With defined values, you will be able to filter out everything that does not align with who you are. This provides a greater sense of confidence in your convictions of your choices and making decisions in both personal and professional situations. Have the courage to make changes if your current circumstances do not align with your values. Eventually, there will be a peaceful flow of positive energy as you begin to align all areas of your life with your core values and live with intention rather than randomly.

The business plan

Goals are a recipe for success. Imagine baking cookies but having no recipe. Your cookies may, by chance, turn out to be edible, yet a much better outcome will most likely be achieved as a result of following the recipe. And to take that one step further, if there is a proven recipe for the best cookies ever baked, by following this recipe, you stand an even greater chance of producing a similarly delicious outcome as well. Success may be thought of in this same way. If you desire to achieve success but do not have a sound plan, by chance, you may achieve a level of success. However, if you take time to research, organize, and prepare a goal, blueprint, or business plan, you will most likely have a much more favorable outcome.

The "one step further" method here would involve selecting someone very successful whom you admire. Learn everything you can about this person. If they have written books, take time to read them. If you know them personally, set up a time to speak with them, ask a substantial number of questions, and listen! Take detailed notes and learn as much as you can. Find out what they have read and where they learned to be successful. Get to know everything you can about this person and the steps they took to become successful. Let them be your recipe or blueprint on your journey of growth and advancement. Learn from the best, and never stop learning.

The following are some of the habits that have helped highly successful people to achieve their goals:[5]

1. *They work hard.* You have to focus on what will truly make you successful, and that is hard work.
2. *They plan.* You must have a strategy that will keep you going and illuminate how to reach your destination.
3. *They take action and don't procrastinate.* Successful people have mastered the habit of taking action.
4. *They have clear goals.* They focus on goals that they know are attainable within a realistic time frame.
5. *They take risks.* Successful people are willing to fail.
6. *They read a lot.* Successful people read and broaden their horizons through the habit of reading.
7. *They do what they are passionate about.* They ensure that their daily habits are centered on activities that will bring out the best in them—and drive them further toward success.

The awareness of my passions led me to the start-up of two new businesses, with the second one meant to help, support, and promote the first one. Upon this new desired path, an aspect revealed immediately along with reprogramming my mind was developing a finely constructed business plan based solely on *my* thoughts. The business plan would include the goals put officially in writing and the methods used to obtain these goals. I researched the elements that encompass a successful business plan and began the undertaking of the creation of this blueprint for success.

With a detailed plan came clarity, understanding, and a vision. I chose to align my thoughts, feelings, and actions with this goal and utilize the power of intention. Spiritually, I believe it is possible to retrain the mind to respond supportively in terms of success, and *energy* is the key. The right kind of energy, that is. Focus should be placed on *positive energy,* and reframing your thoughts to align in response. More about energy will be discussed in Chapter 2.

I have chosen to commit to being successful. I "choose" to be successful. Focusing on this reality has allowed my thoughts to flow continuously toward progress to achieve these goals. These thoughts are both conscious and subconscious. I have set my own realistic, specific, and measurable goals and have a defined time frame in which to achieve them. I recall Brian Tracy saying, *"Feeling listless? Make a list!"*

I have always found this to be true and believe that writing down lists or steps to take to reach certain goals, even and especially on a daily basis, always ensures a most productive outcome. As I allow my goals to grow bigger, I simply need to expand my lists to meet the objectives necessary for advancement.

As your mind becomes focused on a higher goal, a goal that is considered a positive one with pure passionate intentions, your thoughts begin to flood in abundance to create ways to make this new commitment a reality. Whatever you focus and meditate on flows throughout your cells, absorbing energy and causing your thoughts to continually process this object, event, or situation. Often, when you strive to make improvements in your own life, other people become influenced to make positive changes as well.

Gaining an understanding of your mind and how and with what it has been programmed is valuable information to know as you break down the elements of success to its very primal level. We set out to discover a key source of where success does or does not come from, and that is your mind. Every action you take results from how your mind has been programmed and is based on information accumulated since the day you were born. It is always vital to define a problem before any changes can occur. Now that you understand that it is derived from your programming, you are able to begin to rebuild a more meaningful, refined, and accurate pathway to success by developing the backbone of any and every successful business—a business plan including your goals by using your belief system and core values to act as your unconditional guide.

Prayer

Dear Heavenly Father, thank You for today. Thank You for the inspiration You give me to dream and to set goals for myself. I realize I am not guaranteed tomorrow, let alone the rest of today. But setting goals gives me the motivation to live out each day purposefully and with direction. So, I pray that You would help me set my goals and then equip me to fulfill them. I submit each and every goal to You. May my goals reflect Your Will for my life and may they glorify You. I pray for other people who have goals and dreams that they desire to see happen. May You also equip them to reach those precious desires. Fill us with Your awesome purpose in Jesus' name. Amen.[6]

God, help me to achieve my goals and let them be in line with Your plan. If there is an adjustment You would love me to make, God, don't hesitate to let me know so that I won't waste my time chasing the wind. Let Your Will be done. Amen.[6]

Lord, Your Word teaches each of us that it is acceptable to ask for a successful, blessed life. Expand our borders, Precious Lord, and let us find prosperity and success in this gift of life we have been given. You said that You came that we may have life, and that we may have it more abundantly. Please grant us that abundant life, God. Let my life be pleasing to You in all ways, and in all things, so that I will be able to receive the fullness of Your blessings both in this life and in the life to come. Amen.[7]

Reflection

1. Name three things you learned about your mind or your thoughts as you read this chapter.
2. Identify and write down your core values to which you will align all decisions and goals.
3. If you do not already have one, establish a business plan for your current position/business or a future one you have been dreaming about but are hesitant to pursue. Make sure your goals are included and are specific…and lofty!

Wisdom from the Word

> *Commit to the L*ORD *whatever you do,*
> *and He will establish your plans.*
> —Proverbs 16:3 NIV

> *Then their eyes were opened and they recognized*
> *Him; and He vanished from their sight.*
> —Luke 24:31 NASB 1995

> *But blessed is the one who trusts in the*
> *L*ORD, *whose confidence is in him.*
> —Jeremiah 17:7 NIV

CHAPTER 2

Energetically Mindful

What is energy? *Oxford Dictionary* describes energy as *"the strength and vitality required for sustained physical or mental activity."* One of *Merriam-Webster*'s definitions is *"a usually positive spiritual force."* Everything contains energy. All of your cells consist of energy. You can choose what type of energy, positive or negative, you give off into the universe. Your mind consists of energy, and it is in constant motion. If it is programmed to default to negativity, your fruit will align to a pessimistic and constraining environment. But if you capture these thoughts, acknowledge that they are there and they are harmful to your well-being, and then replace them with an empowering substitute, the cells in your body become energized. You have the ability to positively impact the people that surround you. Your energy is infectious, whether positive or negative, so you need to make certain you choose the enlightened path.

What is a vibration? All matter is made up of atoms. There is space between the atoms, and that space allows for movement, known as vibrations. Everything and everyone vibrates. *"When there is frequency, there is electromagnetic potential. We are influenced by the magnetic action of the frequencies that surround us every day, and these frequencies can influence our state of well-being."*[8] For example, you cannot feel joy when you are thinking about the destruction resulting from a devastating hurricane, such as Hurricane Ian, or feel sorrow as you observe the tiny fingers of a precious newborn baby.

You vibrate on either a high, medium, or low level, depending on the emotions you are feeling and your mental state of being. Therefore, your low, medium, or high vibrational thoughts and feelings create reactions with comparable frequencies, resulting in your daily reality.

So, it is important that you understand that your level of vibration is *directly* related to what you are experiencing in your life.

Twelve Ways You Can Help Raise Your Vibration Frequency:

1. *Gratitude.* This is one of the quickest ways to ramp up your vibration. Make gratitude a habit, and it will transform your outlook on life.
2. *Love.* A feeling of expansion, lightness, and happiness will take over your being. Love is one of the highest states of being.
3. *Generosity.* Whatever you want more of in life, offer it out to someone. It *will* come back to you in increase.
4. *Meditation and breathwork.* Train yourself to be present with the moment you are in, as you resonate more harmoniously with the truth. The past and future are only in your mind; you live in the now. This also helps calm your nervous system, improves your mood, and brings about greater feelings of peace.
5. *Forgiveness.* This will release you from low energy. Forgive any injury.
6. *Eat high-vibe food.* Eating local or organic fruits and vegetables makes you feel more light, vibrant, and alive. This high-vibration food makes your personal vibration higher.
7. *Reduce or eliminate alcohol and toxins from your body.* You will feel more energetically abundant by adopting a more healthful and holistic way of life.

8. *Think positive thoughts.* What you think about, you become, and each thought you think affects your future.

9. *Select high-vibe music, television, books, and movies.* Be sure your entertainment is of high vibration and leaves you feeling uplifted rather than depleted.

10. *Surround yourself with beauty.* The right lighting can have a significant impact on your productivity. Be sure your home and work environments reflect beauty, passion, and enthusiasm for life.

11. *Go for a walk outside.* Get some sun on your face as your heart is pumping. Take a break from electronics and technology and reconnect with nature.

12. *Be sure your relationships are "vibing" high.* Surround yourself with people who lift you up rather than drag you down.

> *As you think, you vibrate.*
> —Abraham Hicks

Positive or negative energy?

Did you know that you have the same amount of energy today as you did on the day you were born? Energy doesn't disappear. Conservation of energy is a principle that states that energy can neither be created nor destroyed. But it can be transformed. Energy is constantly changing, altering size, shape, and frequency.

From a business perspective, in my experience, when I have a negative inner world, my career progress is hindered. I have observed that declaring intentions out loud and expressing gratitude have lifted my spirits and grown my positive energy, even to the degree that my business preparations have taken off. Prior to this knowledge, I considered business ideas for months but never took action.

After declaring aloud that my inner world influences my outer world and that I actively choose success in a new business as my goal, it truly felt like positive thoughts flooded my mind, transformed and uplifted my energy, and prompted new ideas and insights. My thoughts led to feelings, and my feelings led to actions, and a twenty-page business plan evolved in less than a week. When you state your intentions out loud, your mind accepts and files this information and is determined to follow through on what you are saying. This is a very effective way to reprogram the files in your mind and allow yourself to confirm your new, bold, and firm successful intentions.

When you are at peace with your inner world, your outer world is a reflection of it. You are able to see difficulties or obstacles as opportunities or possibilities. You remain calm, tranquil, and content, even in the midst of adversity. I trust that as you reprogram your inner world to have faith, confidence, and a gentleness about it, this calmness actually opens your mind up to more possible solutions that a tense and worrisome mind would repress. A problem against achieving inner peace may be wanting to control everything and everyone, as this is a human nature issue. It is necessary to know when to let go. Learn from past experiences and refuse to dwell on them.

Seven Compelling Benefits of Inner Peace:[9]

1. *High self-esteem and confidence.* You will be able to properly think and take action when you feel peace, contentment, and calm within you. You will be in a clearer state of mind when faced with adversity.

2. *A calm soul.* Inner peace allows calmness and tranquility to penetrate to your soul. A calm soul will develop the required character and patience to face difficult circumstances. A peaceful conscience acts as a positive magnet that contributes to positive outcomes.

3. *Eradicating mental and physical health issues.* Inner peace helps to ward off mental health issues, such

as depression, anxiety, and stress. It can also diminish or even prevent physical health problems, such as a racing heart rate or high blood pressure.

4. *Happy and joyful life.* As inner peace helps promote a healthy body, this, in turn, is crucial for a happy and joyful life. You start experiencing more and more happy moments in life.

5. *Reduces negativity.* Negative thoughts may lead to negative energy transformation. Inner peace teaches you to reframe negative thoughts and to always think positively.

6. *Discipline and focus.* Inner peace helps you to focus and concentrate on personal goals and ambitions. Living a disciplined way of life is much easier for a tranquil mind than a conflictual one.

7. *Enlightenment.* Achieving inner peace can almost represent near enlightenment in life. You learn how to eradicate stress, depression, anxiety, and tension from your life.

In my career, I have learned that the more I am aware of my thoughts and only focus on what is helpful, productive, or useful, the more my mind opens up to solutions, opportunities, and possibilities. Rather than limiting my options to a desk job or undesirable "boxed" position, I opened my mind to a new world of opportunities and intriguing possibilities. I chose an office space without walls and continued only to entertain ambitions geared toward growth and success. There is nothing wrong with a desk job or boxed position. The point here is to realize what it is that *you* love to do. Whatever position or career that may be, you must align your goals with your thoughts and focus on making that your reality.

There are times when I have allowed myself to become aware of my own thoughts and discovered how many were negative, critical, wedged in the past, or based on some form of fear—time constraints, circumstances, other people, etc. These are dense low-frequency vibrational thoughts. When I realized how many things or people had the authority to live rent-free in my mind, I "ceased and assisted" in kicking out all the unwanted tenants and replaced them with chosen, encouraging, success-based, light, and hope-filled thoughts.

It is easy to allow the negative circumstances you encounter to weigh you down. It is harder to rise above the challenges and obstacles, which always seem eager to surface or resurface, with a negative demeanor and opposing energy. However, it is worth the extra effort to capture, acknowledge, then replace the negative thoughts; discover what is good and helpful, and perceive every situation as an opportunity to learn, grow, and advance spiritually, mentally, emotionally, and financially. And as you continue to pursue these empowering thoughts, it becomes easier and easier to obtain and maintain them. As written in John 16:33 (NKJV), "*These things I have spoken to you, that in Me you may have peace. In the world you* will *have tribulation; but be of good cheer, I have overcome the world.*"

I am able to look back at my financial career and see that during times of wavering and dense negative vibes, I unknowingly hindered further levels of progress, growth, and success. Have you ever or even recently allowed heavy low-frequency negative thoughts to take control of your mind in the workplace? Or even in your personal life, which affected your decisions or ability to concentrate at your workplace? There is a direct correlation between your negative energy and undesirable or unnecessarily difficult results. It is within your power to choose a focused and uplifted mindset. You are now in control of your level of success, and you are discovering where you want to take it. This frame of mind will lead you down exciting and fruitful paths you never imagined possible.

I have often spent too much time in the business world focused on my financial outcome. Naturally, this is a desired outcome. However, this itself drew on a negative form of pressure to obtain. By redirecting my focus to the *processes* I was completing and disassociating any negative connotation due to pressure, I was able to enjoy the journey and open my mind to new ideas, increase performance, and complete tasks quicker, all leading to higher energy vibes and even greater outcomes. The key was to dissociate the pressure from the process and proceed to succeed. Have you ever experienced a time when you put unwarranted pressure on yourself regarding a work decision or deadline, resulting in a negative outcome due to the negative vibes associated with it? How about in your personal life? Think of an example of each, and observe how you felt in each scenario.

I have also experienced some negative incidents involving money in my past. It is amazing how many people believed my money should be theirs. I often wonder if others have ever felt this way or been in a similar situation. It seemed the harder I worked for it, the more people would be following me with their hands out, reaching for it. This was not concerning a giving or serving type of situation, but rather they were looking to take what did not belong to them from a self-seeking perspective.

Have you ever been in a situation like this? It could even be in the form of extra fees, surcharges, "padded" prices because of where you live, a title you carry, or an overcharge of interest. One case in particular for me was a "friend" who thought he deserved my money. I made a choice to let go of the bitter feelings tied to this that were only hurting me. There's a way of righting wrongs and filling voids that are created. Once I released the negative thoughts and feelings tied to this event, positive thoughts and high-frequency energy, all beneficial to my success, productivity, and abundance, filled the void. I am energized by such a calm and peaceful disposition, and you will be too. It is important to know when to let go of bitter feelings.

Negative energy

You are always in a state of emitting and receiving energy from the things that surround you. Every person, animal, and thing in the universe contains different degrees of positive or negative energy. Negative energy may lead to poor sleep habits, declining health, feelings of anxiety or depression, fatigue, and restlessness, among other unfavorable factors. There may be a lack of desire or motivation to do things you normally find pleasurable. Other people with negative energy may drain *your* energy as well.

This negative energy may be derived from a cluttered or disorganized environment, critical self-talk, or the preprogramming of negative thoughts and memories from your past experiences. Negative energy may even cause harmful health ailments such as headaches, migraines, high blood pressure, and heart disease.

> *Let all bitterness and wrath and anger*
> *and clamor and slander be put away*
> *from you, along with all malice.*
> —Ephesians 4:31 ESV

Negative energy may be spread from person to person in the form of jealousy, pride, gossip, feelings of bitterness or hatred, or other forms of intentionally negative vibes. It is important to protect yourself from these contagious and harmful influences of energy. Being in the presence of continuously negative energy may cause you to feel fatigued, unambitious, fearful, depressed, and angry, and it may even begin to impact your ability to heal.

Negative people are insecure, complainers, judgmental, and rarely turn down an opportunity to put others down. They stir up feelings of sadness, loneliness, rejection, inadequacy, anxiety, and even insecurity. If their image of reality is negative by focusing on a pessimistic worldview, and all the bad things that "could" happen, they cannot help but radiate negative energy into their immediate surroundings.

Positive energy

While energy isn't something we can see, we can certainly *feel* it! "*Good energy can boost our feelings of well-being, dissolve anxiety and improve communication.*"[10] You are a living energy field and have the opportunity to radiate positive energy to others. Have you ever met someone for the first time and could feel their intense positive energy all around you? You instinctively feel good, happy, safe, motivated, energized, and relaxed around these people, benefiting from their positive vibes. On the other hand, have you ever been around someone and could feel the exhaustive and anxious negative vibes enveloping you from just being in their presence? In return, your energy, whether good or bad, will impact the people you are in contact with. *"While your energy is a combination of your past, mindset, dominant thoughts, and perception of the world, at one point you need to take responsibility for the present moment and if needed, work on shifting your energy."*[10]

It is beneficial to be connected to your own emotional health. The better you are at managing this, the better your relationships will tend to be. Emotional energy is contagious, so you must be aware of not only what you are giving off but also what you are receiving from others.

> *So, what if, instead of thinking about solving*
> *your whole life, you just think about adding*
> *additional good things. One at a time.*
> *Just let your pile of good things grow.*
> —Rainbow Rowell

High-frequency energy

Did you know that it's not a lack of energy that makes you feel depleted or an abundance of energy that makes you feel elevated? Instead, it is the *frequency* vibration of the energy that causes these feelings. Since you already know that energy can be neither created nor destroyed, how do you get high-frequency energy? Also mentioned previously was the fact that energy is constantly transformed. It changes its form *"in, through and around you. It changes frequency, and size. Energy can expand and also contract."*[11] It also changes in its molecular structure! People with high-frequency energy inevitably make you feel a great extent of energy in their presence. The reason is that their energy has begun to mix with yours. Signs of high-frequency energy include feeling happy, joy-filled, loving life, appreciative, and excited. Opportunities fall into your lap, and you enjoy loving relationships and are inspired by an optimistic future.

"The frequency of your own energy is determined by your vibration and it all begins with a thought."[11]

> *A cheerful heart is good medicine, but*
> *a crushed spirit dries up the bones.*
> —Proverbs 17:22 NIV

Ways to change your frequency

When you are "feeling" depleted of energy, meaning having a low-frequency vibration rather than having less energy, it's time to take action. Begin with your thoughts. Change your focus. Isolate all negative thoughts, acknowledge them, reframe them, and replace them. Declutter your mind by acknowledging and addressing unresolved thoughts, and declutter your environment physically by organizing and tidying up. If your mind is cluttered with tasks you need to do or things you don't want to forget, take them off your mind by writing them down. Organize them and give them a schedule or a plan to be addressed.

Practice meditation, including special breathing techniques and mind-clearing exercises. Listen to relaxing music and address any invading health issues. Make yourself aware of the current status of your energy, and focus on raising it to a high-frequency level. Elevate your mood and fill your mind with positive, uplifting, and empowering thoughts. Focus on the fruit of the Spirit. *"But the fruit of the Spirit is love, joy, peace, forbearance, kindness, goodness, faithfulness, gentleness and self-control. Against such things there is no law"* (Galatians 5:22–23 NIV). This is the result of the work of the Holy Spirit. Romans 8:6 (NIV), also teaches that *"the mind governed by the flesh is death, but the mind governed by the Spirit is life and peace."* Cleanse negative thoughts from your mind, address what you can, and choose to focus on these spiritual gifts.

"Everything has a frequency including illness and the lower the frequency you are, the more dense or heavier in matter you become. This makes you a perfect Petrie dish for illness to hang around in."[11]

This in itself is reason enough to be aware of your ability to shift the frequency of your own energy. Stay focused on high-frequency energy for your health, success, and happiness. Choose a high-frequency diet, and fill your body with foods of high frequency. The foods that align the most with a high-frequency vibe are nutrient-rich, organic foods, like raw fruits, vegetables, and wild fish. Avoid low-vibrational foods such as processed sugars, artificial sweeteners, grains, and white flour, to name a few. Be mindful of how you feel when you eat different foods. Bless your food, and raise its vibrations.

If you aren't actively raising your vibration, your vibration is declining. You may have heard an old saying, "*If you're not growing, you're dying.*" This is true in a vibrational sense as well. Your energy is constantly changing, and you need to be aware of it and focus on elevating it, even when you feel challenged. You should choose love and light and raise the vibrations to a higher level. If you feel weighed down and are observing the low-frequency, heavy vibes, you have the power to raise the level higher and higher.

A great way to refocus your energy and awareness on love is to harmonize and balance your mind, body, and spirit, which is called coherence. "*Heart coherence is when your brain waves and the waves of your heart are synchronized and move together in an organized manner. When you're in a state of coherence, not only are your heart and mind in alignment, but your cardiovascular system, immune system, hormones, and nervous system are all working together in a harmonious and efficient manner.*"[12] The power of love may positively affect healing, and when all of these systems are in alignment, your entire being will function better.

Take time each day, preferably even several times a day, to perform this meditation. Close your eyes and focus on your breathing. Feel your heart and mind come together in sync. Focus on the words such as love and light in your mind and heart. Repeat words of this kind, such as *Jesus, love, light,* and *angels.* "Fill my energy with love. Fill me with light." Imagine an aura of light surrounding you, growing brighter and brighter. Choose every thought carefully, and only select high-energy, high-vibration light thoughts. Choose peace, joy, serenity, calmness, and self-control. Feel the light energy expand around you. Let it flood your heart, mind, and entire body with positive high-frequency energy, and let it flow into your surroundings. If a negative thought comes to mind, let it flow through you, but do not let it attach to anything. Refocus on positive, loving things and visualize the bright light and the powerfully positive energy surrounding you and lifting you up. Continue this for ten to fifteen minutes.

Energy frequency affects every area of your life. It is best to let go of all negative, bitter, and heavy feelings holding you back, whether it involves money, a toxic relationship, or any unfavorable feeling in general. If you release all ties to these heavy feelings and free your mind to the powerful, light, and rich essence it craves, your life will become more productive, enriched, and useful to yourself as well as those you love. You are able to be better, love more, and live a more fulfilling life.

> *Be careful what you think, because*
> *your thoughts run your life.*
> —Proverbs 4:23 NCV

Energy is an entity of nature that is transferred and transformed yet can neither be created nor destroyed. It flows through all people and throughout the universe. As energy is a needed element in our actions for our transformation, it is important to understand different types of energy and vibrations and how they can be harnessed and utilized in a productive and meaningful way. It is also important to manage your energy as the energy you exhibit affects your perceptions and radiations. This chapter defined and identified differing states of energy and ways to alter the frequency of it to the best form for creative, valuable, useful, and powerful actions.

Prayer

> *Dear God, thank You for this moment in*
> *which I connect with You and Your Infinite Power.*
> *As I read this, my energy, which is really Your*

energy, attains a higher vibration that fills my body, mind and emotions. I am filled with Your energy, O God, and it is Divine. I feel Your energy building within me. Strong and pure, it is unstoppable. Limitless, Your love builds and builds within me. Stronger and stronger, everything it touches is transformed. All illness, all fatigue is washed away, as in a Holy storm. I am new and renewed, my body humming with the joy imprint of Your touch. My increased vibration imparts amazing power to my intentions. The power of my mind is multiplied exponentially by all who read and speak this prayer. As my energy rises, so does the energy of humanity's collective consciousness. Together we speak now as one gigantic and irresistible force, a force for good as we affirm our intention to rise higher. Together, we are stronger and more powerful than any lower energy field can ever be. United with You, we are an unstoppable force of joy! As our spirits rise, the energy of humankind makes a quantum leap into energy fields of love, healing, abundance, joy, wisdom and peace. This level of energy, which is closer to You, has miraculous effects on us and the world. We are held in Your arms as we make this transition. We feel the increase in positive energy and it feels wonderful. We are soothed and comforted. Elated and filled with new life, we make choices aligned with Your love. And as I am drawn to thoughts and activities that strengthen my Divine Connection with You, my life is energized with new, exciting purpose. I wake each day in joy and authentic dedication. I am safe in progressing to a more joyful level where I know everything is possible in You, O God. I affirm that Jesus said: "Ask and you shall receive; knock and the door shall open." All doors to joyful living are now flung open. I radiate joy through my smile. My energy is an unstoppable force of good, for You and my Source. I vibrate at the level of love and Divine Power. My mind is clear. I rise each day full of joy, energy and gratitude. I know how to live today and every day in greatest glory to You. Thank you, God, for this gift that feels so wonderful. I love my life, and I have abundant energy to live it. And so, it is. Amen.[13]

Reflection

Peace results from allowing the Holy Spirit to work in our hearts and minds. When we have peace, we are free from fear and worry and are secure in our eternal salvation.

1. Identify three negative beliefs or thoughts that emanate negative energy when you dwell on them. Acknowledge them, and reframe them to true reality. Now replace these thoughts with a positive twist.
2. Make yourself aware of the type of energy that regularly surrounds you. What type is most common? If it's negative energy, identify a trigger you will use to bring awareness to this negative energy.
3. How will you reframe it to positive energy?
4. Name three things you can do to raise your energy to a high-frequency vibration right now.

Wisdom from the Word

I have told you these things, so that in Me you may have peace. In this world you will have trouble. But take heart! I have overcome the world.
—John 16:33 NIV

Jesus said to him, *I am the way, and
the truth, and the life. No one comes
to the Father, except through Me.*
                              —John 14:6 ESV

*He gives strength to the weary, and to him
who lacks might He increases power.*
                              —Isaiah 40:29 NASB 1995

CHAPTER 3

Consciously Enlightened

Higher level of consciousness

I have been told by a very beloved friend of mine, Kevin, to "*put your praise on*" as I would drift toward feeling like a victim. Each time I shifted my mindset to focus on being grateful for all the amazing things there are to be thankful for, rather than self-pity for something that ultimately ended up being so small or a fear that was not actually there, my spirit and energy were transformed and elevated. This positive energy continued to spread to my immediate surroundings. This was a result of shifting to a higher level of consciousness.

With a higher level of consciousness, which is another way of saying a higher level of awareness, comes a higher level of understanding. Your view of the world will begin to alter. You will own your own feelings and be accountable and responsible for all of your actions, including the past. Your energy will soften, and you will no longer rely on others for your happiness. You will show more compassion and find joy in helping others. Kindness will prevail. You will not fear obstacles or blame others for your misgivings. You will see your imperfections as opportunities for growth and learning. You realize "the Source" of true contentment and success. You enjoy quiet time alone with yourself and find it as an opportunity to regroup and gain further understanding of yourself. You let go of the noise of anger or hostility and focus on a state of peaceful tranquility.

There will be no appeal in the drama of all the "outrage" that comes from news sources. You will learn to avoid dramatic manipulation of the media, as well as that of toxic people. You will lose the appeal of short-term gratifications and focus on long-term healthy goals. You will even become more efficient as you eliminate your old distractions and find clarity in your dreams and desires. A higher level of awareness will lend to extreme feelings of appreciation and gratitude, leaving no room for a negatively competitive nature. You will become at peace with yourself and see a bigger picture in life. The pettiness and destructive habits will dissolve, and a new, fresh, vibrant self will be exposed. This journey to mindfulness affects your mind, body, and soul, mentally and physically.

While the ideation of "consciousness" is speculative, debatable at best, and unresolved from a scientific perspective, what we do know for certain is how powerful our thoughts are. Proverbs 4:23 (NCV) tells us, *"Be careful what you think, because your thoughts run your life."* Think of consciousness as awareness, understanding, mindfulness, or even observation.

A higher level of thinking involves a deeper level of understanding. Life is a journey through different levels of observation. Some say there are six degrees of awareness throughout your lifetime.

Six Levels of Higher Consciousness:[14]

1. Life happens *to* you.
2. Life happens *by* you.
3. Life happens *in* you.
4. Life happens *for* you.
5. Life happens *through* you.
6. Life *is* you.

The first level of observation: life happens to you

The more unobservant you are, the more you feel like a victim to life. You feel like life is happening *to* you. *"When you live in the belief that life is happening to you, you often view it as a possible threat."* You stay caught in your head and try to figure everything out.

The second level of observation: life happens by you

You believe you can take charge of your life at this level rather than be the victim. It can be empowering as you move away from being a victim. This level requires much effort as you believe it is up to you to make things happen. While some aspects of life can be controlled, you cannot influence all the powerful forces involved.

The third level of observation: life happens in you

At this level, you begin to realize that rather than experiencing life, you mostly *think* about it, seeing simply thoughts in your head. Life is experienced through your thoughts. *"We don't see things as they are. We see them as we are,"* says French author Anais Nin. In this phase, you realize that your suffering doesn't come from your life experiences. But rather, it comes from your *stories about* what is happening. Healing can be affected by the choices you make and the beliefs you think and speak.

The fourth level of observation: life happens for you

At this level, you begin to show up for life exactly as it is. Resisting the pains in life turns into more suffering. Here you bring your attention to your experience, whatever that may be. *"Life is not a random series of events. It is a highly intelligent unfolding."* Life is speaking to you at all moments.

The fifth level of observation: life happens through you

You recognize that life is trustable, although not always like-able. You open up to life, even if you are faced with challenges. Life can now move freely through you. You realize that all that has happened to you has been a part of your journey. You move through it rather than reacting to it or trying to control it.

The sixth level of observation: life is you

You are no longer a separate being, but rather you merge completely into union with the body of Christ.

> *You will keep in perfect peace Him*
> *whose mind is stayed on you.*
> —Isaiah 26:3 ESV

> *Finally, brothers, whatever is true, whatever is*
> *honorable, whatever is just, whatever is pure,*
> *whatever is lovely, whatever is commendable,*
> *if there is any excellence, if there is anything*
> *worthy of praise, think about these things.*
> *What you have learned and received and*
> *heard and seen in me—practice these things,*
> *and the God of peace will be with you.*
> —Philippians 4:8-9 ESV

Rather than resisting and controlling, become interested in what you are experiencing at any given moment. Practice elevating your mind with thought-filled awareness of God as "the Source" of all life.

Praise

Living a life of praise is one of the most powerful ways to change your life. There are many benefits to the power of praise. Praise has the ability to lighten your burdens as you raise your spirits to His mighty power. Your burdens are lessened, as well as guilt, frustration, and disappointments. Praise alleviates anxiety by allowing your heart and mind to remain in Christ Jesus. Greater confidence is found by praising God, knowing His ability is greater than any problem. Praise also gives you a stronger intimacy with God and His assurances. Praise with prayer is an even more powerful approach. You experience a heightened awareness of His presence through praise. Many things that overwhelm you will be overshadowed by His immensity if you turn to Him in praise.

Praise also has the transforming power to release grace. With a faith-filled attitude, even a heavy burden or the weight of depression can be lifted. Praise not only affects you, but it also affects the devil and God.[15] It touches every part of your life. *"Likewise, a lack of praise affects you in a negative way, turns the devil loose in your life, and doesn't bless God. You have to get this area of your life right."* Praise is also a great way to counter the culture we live in, where the ungodly are becoming more and more prominent. *"If we don't live lives that are constantly giving thanksgiving and praise unto God, we are not spiritually healthy."* Even if you don't feel joy at all times, you are commanded to speak forth praise to God in faith. *"Learning to praise God even when everything is going badly will change our hearts, make us much more effective, and cause our faith to abound."*[15]

> *Rejoice in the LORD always; and*
> *again I will say, rejoice.*
> —Philippians 4:4 NASB

> *Enter into His gates with thanksgiving, and*
> *into His courts with praise: be thankful*
> *unto Him, and bless His name.*
> —Psalm 100:4 KJV

Praise will get your focus where it needs to be: on God. When you saturate your prayers with praise, you become more focused on the one with the answers rather than being consumed with your problem. It is very difficult for darkness to exist while raising your heart, mind, and spirit in praise. Praise ignites faith and trust in God despite your circumstances. Praise changes your outlook on life.

Gratitude

What is gratitude? *"Gratitude is a positive emotion that involves being thankful and appreciative and is associated with several mental and physical health benefits."*[16] This involves a feeling of gratefulness for someone or something and creates feelings of warmth, kindness, and generosity. Gratitude generally has a positive impact on both physical and psychological health. It may promote better sleep, increased self-esteem, less stress or anxiety, healthier relationships, and even promotes better immunity. Often a grateful person is more likely to be energized to focus on other health-promoting behaviors as well, leading to an overall healthier lifestyle. *"Gratitude blocks toxic emotions, such as envy, resentment, regret, and depression, which can destroy our happiness,"* says Robert Emmons, professor at UC Davis.

Gratitude has an important role in your relationships and your career. *"Cultivate the habit of being grateful for every good thing that comes to you, and to give thanks continuously. And because all things have contributed to your advancement, you should include all things in your gratitude"* (Ralph Waldo Emerson). You will benefit from the practice of expressing gratitude for your life and all it consists of, including the challenges.

Research has shown that there are many benefits to practicing gratitude. It has even been said that success *starts* with gratitude. It can lead to increased happiness, leading to motivation to achieve goals. And gratitude can be contagious. This could be a repetitious cycle of gratitude—motivation—success, repeat. If you find yourself slipping into a slump, remember this loop of success and start practicing gratitude again. It is a repeatable process that can be used at any time.

Gratitude enlightens the spirit and promotes well-being, creating an impact on that moment. It adjusts your perspective, allowing you to realize there is someone bigger than you. Grateful people are more motivated and programmed to achieve more and even pay forward their positive energy and gratitude to others. It is a desirable trait to have for both business and personal relationships. Grateful people sleep better, are more resilient to challenges, and are mentally and physically healthier in general.

"Gratitude is different from other caring emotions such as sympathy and compassion because it's learned…taking the time to appreciate what you have is one of the keys to cultivating gratitude."[17] It involves taking the time to express appreciation and return kindness. Having an attitude of gratitude should be a lifelong pursuit. You can train your brain to focus less on negative thoughts and become more aware of positive thoughts. Start by simply acknowledging small moments throughout the day as they happen. Learn to appreciate how far you have come and the opportunities that lie ahead. Practice mindfulness throughout the day as well, smile and make gratefulness a priority. The simple act of showing gratitude has a powerful effect on happiness, motivation, and ultimately success. Engaging in praise, appreciation, complimenting, and showing gratitude are methods that all lead to success.

Net worth

Praise and gratitude are both very important aspects that can help you not only grow your character but also grow your net worth. Net worth is an overall picture of your financial health. It is a snapshot of your current financial position. It can be figured out by adding up all of your assets, including cash in bank accounts, investments, retirement accounts, properties you own (primary and investment homes), etc. Then subtract any debt or liabilities you have or owe. Simply put, it is all that you own minus all that you owe.

When assessing your financial stability, it is more important to consider your net worth rather than actual dollars or income. Income is not always predictable. Tracking your net worth can help you understand where your money has gone and where you want it to go presently and in the future.

Ten Key Reasons Why You Need to Know Your Net Worth:[18]

1. *Key benchmark.* Net worth is an important benchmark that measures your household's successes.

2. *Set goals.* Net worth is essential in order to set your immediate and long-term goals. Income is not always predictable, but steady growth of net worth is still possible with proper planning.

3. *Track progress.* Track changes in your net worth as early as possible to ensure progress in managing your money properly.

4. *An emergency fund is essential.* You should always plan an emergency fund for unforeseen circumstances, such as a lost job or medical misfortune. Have liquidity available for easy and quick access to funds if needed.

5. *For borrowing.* By having net worth calculated, you are better able to assess your status when making decisions on things such as buying a house, college tuition, or investing in a new business, so you are able to see what you can afford. Lending facilities will require an assessment of this as well.

6. *Pay off debt.* You are better able to pay down high-yielding debt with the bigger picture in mind.

7. *Refinance mortgage debt.* You are also able to have a better grasp on mortgage debt and repayment.

8. *Build assets.* Take full advantage of adding to your retirement accounts and your employer's match, and increase investments in a low-cost index fund. Focus on building your investments wherever possible.

9. *Financial planning.* Your road map to building wealth starts with knowing your net worth and making valuable changes like reduced spending, increased saving, and investing. It enables you to make adjustments to your budget, knowing where your finances stand.

10. *Financial security.* Knowing your net worth is having a tool to measure your financial security at any point in time. There are even apps that can help you build your net worth, track spending, etc.

I believe that where you focus your mind, energy will follow. And I choose to direct positive, optimistic energy toward growth in business, personally, spiritually, and even financially. As Napoleon Hill states, *"Focus on the possibilities for success, not on the potential for failure."* All energy is focused on success.

I admire all types of people, especially those who have taken the time, with devotion and ambition, to become successful. These people most likely show success in most, if not all, areas of their lives as they are motivated and refuse to allow *failure* in their vocabulary. I bless these people and all of their efforts and am thrilled for the resulting success they have achieved. They are inspiring and make for excellent role models.

You have the ability to change what you are thinking. If you incorporate praise and gratitude into your daily life and focus on what you want rather than what you don't want, this change likely will occur. To build financial independence, it's important to focus on building net worth more so than growing income. The tax rate will also be lower as the government looks at income rather than wealth or net worth. In addition, income may not always be certain as job security isn't always a dependable factor. Therefore, focusing on growing net worth is a wise way to build and secure an abundant and healthy financial future.

You are the designer of your thoughts, so you need to focus on what you want. The ultimate measure of wealth is considered to be net worth, as it can be turned into cash if/when needed. Although income is important, it is only a portion of the whole net worth equation. There are many ways to add to net worth, such as income, savings, investments, appreciating asset accumulation, and even passive income. Choosing a variety of sources provides more avenues to build upon. By focusing positive thoughts on growing your net worth and faithfully recognizing God as the Source, expanding benefits will result. As mentioned previously, where attention goes, energy flows, and action will result.

When you exhibit praise and gratitude, your body exudes positive energy, and it is proven to work much more efficiently. In a pleasant environment, people foster positivity, high productivity, and even happiness. It is, therefore, important to cultivate a positive mindset. And *"one positive thought produces millions of positive vibrations"* (John Coltrane). And positive vibrations are linked to good health, happiness, and abundance.

As you prepare to reprogram your mind to a new empowering way of thinking for success, reaching a higher level of consciousness is necessary in order to receive a deeper level of understanding. This chapter defined the different levels of observation and how you may feel and live life at each level. You are able to observe your current level of awareness and show yourself the options of where you might rather be. You also learned the riveting effects and priceless value of praise and gratitude when incorporated into your daily interactions. If incorporated into all aspects of your life, they will inevitably be a driving force leading to prosperity as you maximize your net worth, knowing this is a crucial benchmark at any particular time. It will provide the best road map to building your wealth.

Prayer

> *Almighty God, I owe all my accomplishments to You alone. There's nothing I have achieved that didn't come from You. You gave me all I have today; that's why I have come to say thank You with gratitude overflowing from the heart. I praise You and will always praise You for my success story and those that are yet to come. LORD, assist me in maintaining an attitude of gratitude every day of my life. In Jesus' name I pray, Amen.*[19]

Dear Heavenly Father, I worship You because You are Almighty God. You are worthy of my praise each day. Thank You for Your faithfulness to me, whatever I'm going through in my life. Forgive me for forgetting to worship You in a way You deserve. I want to offer my best praise for who You are. The more I worship You, LORD, the more I sense Your presence in my life. You are a merciful and loving Father. I praise the name of Your son, Jesus, who died so that those who believe can have eternal life with You. Thank You for that amazing promise. You are awesome and wonderful. In Jesus' name I pray, Amen.[20]

Dear God, I decree, in Jesus Christ's name, that vast improvement is coming quickly in every phase of my life. Every day, in every way, things are getting better and better for me. I now let go of worn-out conditions and ways of living life. Abundance is flowing. It is on the move. Abundance is flowing to me in increasing amounts. The money I now hold is blessed with Your energy. The money I spend circulates, doing every kind of good. The money I give returns to me greatly multiplied. I now consent with my human mind, to Your Divine Mind and asked to be programmed exclusively for prosperity. I desire abundant living. I know that I deserve abundance, and, as Your child, I claim it.

Dear God, I do not think it is a virtue to be poor, and I know I am worthy of ever-increasing abundance. More and more abundance is coming about easily and effortlessly. I visualize all my bills paid. I visualize having enough, with money to spare.

Dear God, in my human mind, I accept that abundance is good, especially in its rightful place. I am beautifully and appropriately supplied, clothed, housed, and transported with rich substance of the Divine now.

God, as Your beloved child, I consent to a good life, well and happy in every phase of my life. From this moment forward, I decree, in Jesus Christ's name, that You, dear God, will provide a continuous flow of good into my life. This is the hour when the change occurs and I become an irresistible magnet for prosperous people and experiences. With all my heart, I believe. I dissolve from my mind any idea that prosperity can be withheld from me.

Dear God, I am Your child, and I consent to receive. I am receiving all the wealth You have for me now. In Jesus Christ's name I pray. Amen.[21]

Exercise

Close your eyes and focus on your breathing. Feel your heart and mind come together in sync. Focus on words such as love and light in your mind and heart. Repeat words of this kind, such as *Jesus*, love, *light*, and *angels*. "Fill my energy with love. Fill me with light." Imagine an aura of light surrounding you, growing brighter and brighter. Choose every thought carefully and only select high-energy, high-vibration light thoughts. Choose peace, joy, serenity, calmness, and self-control.

Feel the light energy expand around you. Let it flood your heart, mind, and entire body with positive high-frequency energy, and let it flow into your surroundings. If a negative thought comes to mind, let it flow through you, but do not let it attach to anything. Refocus on positive, loving things, and visualize the bright light and powerfully positive energy surrounding you and lifting you up.

Reflection

1. Spend three times today praising God for your outcomes or circumstances, whether good or unfavorable. Continue this on a daily basis. The more times, the better.

2. Name seven things today you are grateful for. Now praise God for each of them. Repeat daily.
3. Identify your current level of consciousness. Is this where you want to be? If it isn't, what will you do today to change it?
4. If you haven't already, develop an Excel file or find an app to track your net worth. Keep a running tab and make adjustments weekly or monthly as necessary. Revisit monthly, and give it focus and energy.

Wisdom from the Word

> *Consider it pure joy, my brothers and sisters,*
> *whenever you face trials of many kinds, because*
> *you know that the testing of your faith produces*
> *perseverance. Let perseverance finish its work*
> *so that you may be mature and complete, not*
> *lacking anything. If any of you lacks wisdom,*
> *you should ask God, Who gives generously to all*
> *without finding fault, and it will be given to you.*
> —James 1:2–5 NIV

> *Great is the L*ORD *and most worthy of*
> *praise; His greatness no one can fathom.*
> —Psalm 145:3 NIV

> *Do not be anxious about anything, but in*
> *every situation, by prayer and petition, with*
> *thanksgiving, present your requests to God.*
> *And the peace of God, which transcends*
> *all understanding, will guard your hearts*
> *and your minds in Christ Jesus.*
> —Philippians 4:6–7 NIV

CHAPTER 4

Skillfully Managed

Education

Learning is a lifelong process and is the key to success and more opportunities in your life. It is so important to focus a good deal of time on educating yourself. Read about something related to your career daily. Read about investments. Read documentaries. Read books in your field. Read everything educational you can get your hands on. It is so easy to find numerous methods of education today.

There are audio memberships you could join for continuous learning. Get to know your local library as an amazing resource. Many have created an online venue or even their own app, in which you can download e-books and audiobooks for free. Training can be found in the form of online courses for continuing education or certificates. Sign up at a local community college for specific courses in your field or as a supplement to your field. Sign up for webinars online or attend conferences in your area of interest. This allows for networking with like-minded people, expands the level of opportunities, and builds motivation from all of the encouraging and empowering positive energy flowing through passionate and driven people.

Let your vehicle be your university on wheels. Subscribe to podcasts or newsletters. Sign up for emails from an educational source. Find a mentor or seek educational field trips. Read blogs in your field. Reading is fundamental. It is essential and necessary to further develop your education and advance your growth and success. Even reading a good mystery for pleasure stimulates processes in your brain, allowing creativity to flow and the imagination to soar. Strive to know every aspect of your position, and be the best at whatever it is you are doing. Give your best every day and achieve excellence in your work. Encourage those around you to do the same, engaging in educational opportunities and striving for excellence. There is power in numbers; the more people who are aligned with the same passionate and positive goals, the more favorable high-frequency energy will be poured out into your immediate surroundings.

10 Benefits Showing Why Education Is Important to Our Society:[22]

1. *Creating more employment opportunities.* Whether enhancing your own career position or seeking something new, education will increase your chances of landing a desirable and fulfilling job.

2. *Securing a higher income.* Highly educated people are more likely to get high-paying, expert jobs. Your credentials will motivate an employer to choose you over other candidates or your business as a choice client.

3. *Developing problem-solving skills.* Education teaches us how to obtain and develop critical and logical thinking and make independent decisions. It also allows for reliable evidence to back up and confirm decisions.

4. *Improving the economy.* The higher the education and accomplishments, the better the employment options. Education helps grow the economy if you apply it wisely and improve other people's lives as well.

5. *Providing a prosperous and happy life.* Education secures respect from society. It helps gain a better reputation and increases the chances of "climbing the career ladder" more easily and quicker.

Education, leading to higher income, increases the likelihood of buying a home and expands stability and confidence, all thereby creating a more positive environment.

6. *Giving back to the community.* Educated people understand how valuable it is to live in a stable and secure community. It is important to give back and help improve your own neighborhood and community in general. Get involved in order to build a better place for all to live in.

7. *Creating a modern society.* Education molds people into leaders. Competent leaders help guide us down good paths.

8. *Bridging the borders.* Digital education helps connect with people and organizations around the world. Borders are no longer there. Communication is open with other countries.

9. *Creating equal opportunities.* Educated people are treated as equals based on their knowledge and competence. Educated people are more likely to listen and accept other people's points of view.

10. *Introducing empowerment.* Education is the key to turning a weakness into a strength. It offers us considerable mental agility to make good decisions.

Money management

As you progress in your career, it is important to understand how to invest your earnings wisely. Are you saving for a down payment on a house? Or college for children? Or maybe a sporty new car? Being a wise money manager allows you to accumulate savings and gives you control over your finances. People who are successful at managing their money are able to enjoy these and other exciting benefits, such as traveling or being a little frivolous once in a while. Learning how to manage finances so you have a surplus of funds can lead to reduced stress and increased security about the future. And the good news is that money management is a skill that can be learned.

Managing money is a true testament to being responsible and accountable for what you have been entrusted. Part of money management is living within your means. Creating a budget is one of the most important parts of money management within a home. *"A budget is an estimation of expenses and income over a certain period, usually monthly, quarterly or yearly."*[23] Budgeting helps you to understand cash inflows and outflows and keeps you keenly aware of your current financial situation.

Until I started an active budget, I did not realize how many subscriptions, licenses, or memberships I had on auto-renewal. It took a full year of budgeting until all of my expenses truly were exposed. Some people find auto-renewal a helpful tool, and others may not like the idea. Personally, I do not. I like to have complete control over my moneymaking decisions and have the opportunity to rethink whether or not I find another year of the subscription necessary, without the pressure of an automatic payment I may forget about. However, in most situations, you may go into your account and manually remove the automatic renewal option.

There are many different apps and templates for budgeting. I was first introduced to Dave Ramsey's Financial Peace University course back in 2015 and discovered firsthand the value of developing and following a budget by utilizing the EveryDollar budget tool. This tool works on the basis of a zero-based budget, assigning every dollar to a chosen category. I found that it took my budget a few months to evolve and, as I mentioned earlier, as I worked on collecting all sources of income as well as expenses.

Although my budget was well underway by the third month, I had finally collected the last of my unknown auto-renewal data at the one-year mark. This process brought awareness and control of my finances by tracking them and even allowed me to capture more savings potential and spending opportunities with no more surprises.

It is vital to know where your inflow of money and expenses are and to accurately and intentionally tell each dollar where and how to work for you. This is an area that many people struggle with. Budgeting isn't just for people who would like to obtain financial freedom. It is a system for everyone who would like to be in full control of their finances, and know where the money comes from and is going, and it will improve overall financial health. It should become a part of your daily/weekly/monthly planning. Adjust the budget until it fits your current lifestyle and goals. Once it is stable, you will be able to watch your investment opportunities expand, your debt will dissolve, and your net worth will grow.

Budgeting in business is one of the most important parts of having a business. This makes it possible to create an investment strategy and plan for expenditures, employees, continued operations, plus other anticipated and unanticipated costs. Some disadvantages of failing to prepare and follow a budget are overspending, under-performance, and not being prepared for necessary costs or awareness of the heartbeat of the company. Budgeting allows businesses to plan expenses, such as advertising, loans, insurance, professional services, payroll, and other ancillary costs. It also provides peace of mind by properly managing risk by documenting funds set aside for emergencies and visualizing where funds may be diverted from for an unexpected occasion.

Time management

As a person of integrity, you must manage time differently than the secular world. You must first seek God in everything you do. You are to organize your time and plan wisely for the future. *"Time is your most precious gift, because you only have a set amount of it"* (Rick Warren). Seek God daily and allow Him to direct your activities. Avoid placing focus on worldly endeavors. *"Live with an eternal perspective that will lead to managing your time better and doing God's will."*[24]

Money provides options for you to live a better life, putting you in a better position of control over your finances. Having money and successfully managing your finances also gives you freedom and options to decide how you want to live and support the things you care most about in your life. And just as important as money management is time management. Our time is precious. And time is money. There are only so many hours in a day. It is vital to make the most of your time, value it, and use it wisely. You are rewarded favorably when you manage both the time and the money you have been blessed with.

> *Time is the most valuable thing a man can spend.*
> —Diogenes Laertius

Better time management will allow you to start sooner, finish earlier, get there faster, make more, and enjoy better.

> *Time management is not a peripheral*
> *activity or skill. It is the core skill upon*
> *which everything else in life depends.*
> —Brian Tracy

10 Strategies for Better Time Management:[25]

1. *Know how you spend your time.* Log your time for a week or two and evaluate the results. Are you completing what you need to get done? What time of day are you most productive? Where does most of your time go? Are you investing your time wisely?
2. *Set priorities.* Differentiate between what is important and what is urgent. Gain greater control over your time. Create a "to-do" list and rank them in order of priority. This allows you to set boundaries and identify what is most urgent.
3. *Use a planning tool.* This may be a planner, calendar, phone app, notebook, wall chart, or index card. By writing down your tasks and schedules, you free up your mind to focus on your priorities.

4. *Get organized.* Disorganization leads to poor time management. Clutter has a strong negative impact on perceived well-being. Also, being organized will improve the time you spend processing information. Avoid wasting time.

5. *Schedule appropriately.* Be sure to build in time for things you want to do. Plan your most challenging tasks for when you have the highest energy. Block out time for high-priority activities first and guard against interruptions. Allow for creative time as well.

6. *Delegate: get help from others.* Assign responsibility for a task to someone else, freeing up your time for tasks that require your expertise. Be specific and design the task with your expectations. Another way to get help is to "buy" time by obtaining services that save time, such as housecleaning or lawn services.

7. *Stop procrastinating.* Complete the biggest, most urgent tasks first. You could also break the big tasks up into smaller ones that do not seem so overwhelming. Perhaps even build a reward system for completed tasks to help stay motivated.

8. *Manage time-wasters.* Avoid things such as small talk, overscheduling, or unnecessary meetings. Take advantage of things such as voice-to-text features. Follow up on items immediately. Break away from devices when possible.

9. *Avoid multitasking.* Routine multitasking may lead to difficulty in concentrating and maintaining focus. Do your best to focus on one task at a time and keep your area free of distractions. Turn off notifications on your devices, and set aside dedicated time for specific tasks.

10. *Stay healthy.* You are an important investment of time. Schedule time to relax or do nothing. This

enables you to accomplish tasks more quickly and easily. Give your mind time to relax and get proper sleep.

Successful time management leads to greater personal happiness, increased accomplishments, and an abundant future.

Spiritual wealth

Being "rich" spiritually is the wealthiest type of rich possible. This is the ultimate wealth and also the most accessible type of wealth.

> *If we have not developed a reservoir of spiritual wealth, no amount of money is likely to make us happy. Spiritual wealth provides faith. It gives us love. It brings and expands wisdom. Spiritual wealth leads to happiness because it guides us into useful or loving relationships.*
> —John Templeton

> *The marvelous thing about spiritual wealth is that when we take our part in that, everyone else is blessed; whereas, if we refuse to be partakers, we hinder others from entering into the riches of God.*
> —Oswald Chambers

The ability to integrate a rich spiritual life with material possessions is a reflection of your inner world. The power and meaning you give it determines how you value it and live your life.

Passive income

Change your focus from active to passive income. While still earning an active income, brainstorm all the ways possible to add more passive income to your story. Consider commercial real estate, residential real estate, land, rentals, storage facilities, equity invest-ments, numerous online businesses, and so much more. Get creative! Read, study, and watch educational resources to guide and inspire you to expand your income into the passive sector. Spending time on research and education on passive income possibilities is a wise investment guaranteed to produce fruitful results.

> *The most powerful form of wealth-building today isn't about earning a paycheck. It's about what you know.*
> —T. Harv Eker

Passive income doesn't just happen. It takes time, dedication, and life adjustments in order to achieve it. It is also important to enjoy every moment along the journey toward success. Wealth doesn't come solely from what you accumulate in your pockets. True wealth comes from feeling fulfilled and accomplished in everything you do.

> *Passive income does not have to be huge; it just has to give you a little extra money for something that's important in your life.*
> —Wanda Urbanska

Using the money that you currently have to make more money makes good sense. Or even using someone else's money to invest is very wise. This is known as leverage. Consider taking some money that has been set aside for savings and utilizing it to build more money. How about being "the bank" for someone else's project with an interest return on your investment? Naturally, be very careful that a secure agreement is in place in advance.

Rather than let money set without adding value, find ways to make it work for you. Keep in mind to always keep enough liquid for three to six months' worth of expenses in case of an emergency. Robert Kiyosaki takes it one step further to actually focus on passive income *first*. He says, *"I'm a huge believer that starting out with just*

passive sources can really be beneficial to your wealth-building because there are many years where you're going to have low or no active income."
Twelve Benefits of Passive Income:[26]

1. *Lifted income limits.* For active income, you trade time for money, and there is a limit. However, if you make a passive income, you may not have to be physically present to get paid. You can make money day or night, and limits are lifted on how much you can make.
2. *More free time.* While active income involves being physically present and working a required number of hours, passive income allows you to separate your time from your income source.
3. *Ability to be location independent.* There are hundreds of passive income sources that allow you to work or live anywhere.
4. *Better tax breaks.* Often, taxes are higher for employees than for sole proprietors. Also, you can write off some of your business expenses in your personal taxes.
5. *A new form of financial stability.* While with an active income you are at the mercy of your employer, a passive income provides financial stability within your own control. Having multiple streams of passive income that are diversified is an excellent way to add more financial security.
6. *Less work-related stress.* Creating a profitable passive income source will take time, but for those patient and persistent, it can reduce stress, anxiety, and fear for the future once the streams are rolling.
7. *Vacations at your leisure.* As most forms of passive income can be maintained from almost anywhere, you are able to have flexibility in the time and location of your vacation destination.

8. *No getting fired or laid off.* While there are other minor risks involved with passive income, you have the power to quit or continue each venture you start. You are in control of this.

9. *Work on your passions & hobbies.* Having your own passive income source allows you to live from things you are passionate and enthusiastic about.

10. *Create your own retirement plan.* You are able to use the passive income to save for retirement or re-invest in yet another sustainable source of passive income that will still provide long after you have retired. You could also possibly eliminate some of the expenses that an active source of income may accumulate (transportation, gas, time, etc.)

11. *Pursue your dreams.* Set your own goals and strive to achieve them. Do not let life pass you by. It requires hard work, discipline, and motivation, but the rewards are more than just financial.

12. *Personal growth.* When you are building passive income streams, you are able to update and advance your own personal skills and that which interests you.

Think big

While I have spent many of my employment years in the same field that I am good at and educated in, I neglected some of my true talents. These stand out as things that just come naturally or are so enjoyable that they don't even feel like work. I always thought I had to spend my career days working where my diploma pointed. This was thinking small. My eyes have been opened to focus on my talents, what comes easily, and is enjoyable. It took a leap of faith for me to realize I could actually do what I found most enjoyable and pursue this as a profitable career. As Danny Angel says best, *"The secret to happiness is doing what you love and the secret of success is loving what you do.*" This is thinking big.

I used to believe that if I thought big, it might only result in a big disappointment as well. Then I began to pursue the thoughts and actions of successful people. I chose to start thinking big and opened my mind to new possibilities. I love the idea of helping people, and small thoughts do not allow much room for this to transpire. According to Richard Branson, *"If people aren't calling you crazy, you aren't thinking big enough."*

It is time to start thinking big and changing lives! It would seem as though if you thought big and were rewarded for your focused efforts, the right thing to do is pay forward to other people in need. Natural consequences have a way of balancing things out. Do your part and help and serve one another. There will be a day when you have a need for something as well. It all circles back. And no matter what, you cannot overstate the positive and energized feelings that occur simultaneously with the actions of making a favorable impact on someone else's life.

From a business perspective, I extract "rich" as a form of financial wealth and choose to operate from a positive, enlightened, and ambitious frame of mind. I am eager to learn from those who have already figured out how to be successful. I learn from them and model my thoughts after theirs, which ultimately leads to successful actions. Associating with like-minded people and striving to improve is a stepping stone to financial success.

More important to me than being rich financially is being rich personally and spiritually. I continually work to enrich my life and my relationships, especially with family and close friends. I also believe it is important to develop rich relationships with neighbors and extended family, in a church, or a community. Iron sharpens iron, and becoming rich in personal relationships is as sharp as it gets.

Learning and continual education are extremely important to maintaining a healthy career. The more you learn, the more you earn. Knowledge is the key to advancement and promotion. The more you know, the greater the options you will have in a job or position selection, flexibility, financial advancement, and job satisfaction. Create a learning plan. Define business goals of what you hope to be achieved, and make an actionable plan regarding how to support it. Set time aside each day to learn something new to enhance your understanding of your field or business. Technology is advancing rapidly, and you better be able to keep up, or someone else will pass you by.

Personal growth is the improvement of your skills, knowledge, and other personal qualities. This helps you to be the best you can be and live a content and fulfilling life. This may involve a positive mental, physical, and spiritual transformation. This includes learning as well as applying what you learned and reprogramming your mind.

Intimacy with God is the way to true fulfillment, yet other areas of growth include emotional, mental, social skills, spiritual self, and overall health and well-being. Personal growth also leads to a more loving relationship with yourself and others.

Spiritual growth is essential for a better, happier, and a more accordant life, free of fear and anxiety. In this process, you expel the incorrect concepts and beliefs and refine the insights into who you are and the world surrounding you. Through this, you reach a state of inner peace. You build inner strength, and your confidence grows as well. By removing limiting and negative thoughts, you allow positive and supportive energy to flow throughout your mind and body.

> *The path of spiritual growth is a*
> *path of lifelong learning.*
> —M. Scott Peck

Continual learning is a nonnegotiable aspect in the mind of a person striving to be or stay successful. In anything you choose to do, knowledge is power, and the more you grow in wisdom, the greater your opportunities will become and the higher the probability of achieving the success you desire. This chapter covered the imperative nature of education as well as the valuable practice of other leadership skills, such as time and money management and understanding many possible sources of generating passive income.

Passive income is a form of financial freedom. You have the freedom to choose, set, and achieve your own goals and to constantly learn and do what you love. These skills are also vital in growing wealth in abundant proportions. If permitted, they will open your mind to the possibilities you have yet to discover. And, finally, now that you are awakening in consciousness, a spiritual growth mindset supports the intentions to view life from a lens aligned with your belief system for abundance and success. With the power of a spiritual growth mindset, you progress in projecting success that is aligned with your sole purpose.

Prayer

Heavenly Father, thank You for Your provision and for all You have given me to use as a means to live. I pray I will have wisdom as I manage my money and time. Please shape my perspectives and my views about each of these provisions. Teach me how to spend and save each of them. I pray I would hold my money loosely, and my time preciously, to put each of them in their proper perspectives. I also pray that You would be generous with each of them, giving them as You see fit. I pray that You are glorified in how I manage my money and time in Jesus' name.

Almighty Father, I come before You and ask for a financial blessing in the form of passive income. Give me the wisdom to find multiple sources to improve my situation and relieve my financial stress. And Father, You have called me to grow in grace, to increase my understanding of Jesus and to develop a close and intimate relationship with You. LORD, this is what I desire to do, and I pray I may come to know You more and more each day. Increase my spiritual growth. I pray that I may learn to walk in spirit and truth and learn to live godly in Christ Jesus. In Jesus's name I pray. Amen.

Exercise

Close your eyes and focus on your breathing. Feel your heart and mind come together in sync. Focus on words such as love and light in your mind and heart. Repeat words of this kind, such as *Jesus, love, light,* and *angels.* "Fill my energy with love. Fill me with light." Imagine an aura of light surrounding you, growing brighter and brighter. Choose every thought carefully and only select high-energy, high-vibration light thoughts. Choose peace, joy, serenity, calmness, and self-control.

Feel the light energy expand around you. Let it flood your heart, mind, and entire body with positive high-frequency energy, and let it flow into your surroundings. If a negative thought comes to mind, let it flow through you, but do not let it attach to anything. Refocus on positive, loving things and visualize the bright light and powerfully positive energy surrounding you and lifting you up.

Reflection

1. How are you currently managing your money? Find a budget template that appeals to you and work daily on developing a budget that aligns with your lifestyle.
2. Identify three concerns in your current management of time. Write down ideas of changes you will make to improve these concerns.
3. Identify three passive income sources you will begin to focus on, write down, dwell on, and pursue.

Wisdom From the Word

> *Honor the LORD with your wealth and*
> *with the firstfruits of all your produce.*
> —Proverbs 3:9 ESV

> *So, then, be careful how you live. Do not be*
> *unwise but wise, making the best use of your time*
> *because the times are evil. Therefore, do not be*
> *foolish, but understand what the LORD's will is.*
> —Ephesians 5:15–17 ISV

> *Behave wisely toward outsiders,*
> *making the best use of your time.*
> —Colossians 4:5 ISV

CHAPTER 5

Thoroughly Challenged

Obstacles of success

Obstacles will always be a part of your business environment. You would not be growing if they weren't. It is vital to be able to view them as opportunities for growth and to expand your mind to solutions or ways that would not have been possible without any turbulence. When I see every challenging situation as an occasion to brainstorm for creative solutions, my business, as well as my character, have resulted in new, productive, and surprising resolutions. I focus on what I have and can do rather than what I do not have or cannot access.

I have practiced the "ready, fire, aim" method, although my logic was slightly premature. Perhaps the "ready" part wasn't quite developed enough in the preprogramming phase. Now that I have spent time reprogramming my mind with supportive thoughts, leading to corroborative feelings, successful actions have become the result. Therefore, I can "ready, fire, aim" with confidence that adaptation or adjustments will always result in a positive and favorable outcome.

As you often get what you subconsciously want, you should choose to focus on opportunities rather than obstacles. Wherever you focus your energies, your thoughts eventually become programmed into your mind and often lead to results that are aligned.

Our human nature thrives in an optimistic environment. Choose to lift your spirit and focus on elevated energy and positive outcomes. Joe Rogan resembled these beliefs, stating, *"There is a direct correlation between positive energy and positive results."* Reframe everything that is unfavorable in an optimistic light as an opportunity.

It is so important to recognize when your thinking isn't empowering. Put forth effort each day to capture unfavorable and harmful thoughts which have no business in your business. Fill your business mind with empowering and creative thoughts, knowing this is a key to success. Bless your successful business and those who participate in all matters of your surroundings. Also, bless the success of others.

I have found that sales were forced, sparse, and unfulfilling when I attempted to sell products I didn't fully believe in. When I redefined my values and understood who I was and what I represented, I was able to make changes in my businesses, my mindset, and my products. These changes energized all of my efforts and provided confidence in believing in and thus sharing myself and my products. Like-minded people are always eager to join in where enthusiasm abounds.

Physical and mental clutter

Clutter, whether mental or physical, has an unfavorable impact on your well-being. Mental clutter involves an overload of negative thoughts piled into your mind that has not been identified, acknowledged, reframed, replaced, and properly filed in your brain. The result is a negative energy flow into your immediate surroundings. It may also result from too many thoughts in general, whether good or bad, that have not yet been processed.

Mental clutter will most likely lead to feeling overwhelmed, leading to other pessimistic outcomes and energy. Being overwhelmed has a profoundly damaging effect on cognitive function. It is a sign that the brain is overloaded, and you feel out of control. Often at this point, your brain will block connections and signals to disassociate in order to protect itself.

Physical clutter works the same way as mental clutter but is in physical form. Being in an environment surrounded by an overabundance of "stuff" may be overpowering. The clutter leads to feelings of disorganization and distraction and creates the same overwhelming feeling as mental clutter. Physical clutter may have negative mental health consequences. While some people will have a greater tolerance for clutter than others, the overall tendency is increased stress levels, difficulty concentrating, and possible effects on relationships.

Clutter, in general, may also lead to procrastination. Whether it has become difficult to physically sort through piles of papers and bills or to mentally recall the long list of things that need to be addressed, the outcome is generally to delay some sort of action that needs to occur. It is understood that people with cluttered homes, offices, minds, or any other space tend to procrastinate on important tasks.

Clutter may also lead to unwarranted impulses, feelings of a loss of control, and a lower quality of life. Self-esteem and a degree of self-worth are negatively affected when the mind becomes overpopulated with unresolved thoughts. Some people actually find comfort in holding on to clutter mentally or physically. Somehow it is "comfortable" to them, and they hold on to it while it damages them in other ways.

Lack of focus

Lack of focus or clarity is a major obstacle to success. There are many negative consequences that may result, including preventable mistakes, decision-making struggles, low-quality work, unmet deadlines, and lack of team connectedness. Inability or unwillingness to focus could also be costly to your business or company. The first step to combatting this obstacle is identifying the source of lost focus. Is there a personal trigger in your life that is causing you to lose focus? Is there a health-related issue that is the source? What other causes may lead to this lack of concentration? Identifying the cause will begin to put this obstacle in proper perspective.

Proper sleep, eating, and exercise habits may help improve focus. You can also perform concentration exercises to help boost your ability to concentrate. Establishing a serene environment and eliminating distractions will also provide an atmosphere more suitable for concentrating. If possible, reduce multitasking and commit to focusing on one task at a time. Practicing mindfulness and meditation, concentrating on your breathing and thoughts, may make your brain calmer and improve focus. Taking frequent breaks allows the mind to refresh and recharge. Listen to music and practice self-care or perhaps treat yourself to an occasional spa day or tee time. Remove distractions in your environment, such as clutter. Try organizing your space and eliminating unnecessary messes. Learning how to concentrate is essential to succeeding in your business or career.

Values are very important to represent who you are. A standard of values should be steady and even-keeled, emanating through all aspects of your life—professionally, personally, financially, and spiritually. I place a high value on all of my relationships and am proud to promote my own value to others and respect and value them as well.

> *True greatness is not measured by the*
> *headlines a person commands or the wealth*
> *he or she accumulates. The inner character*
> *of a person—the undergirding moral and*
> *spiritual values and commitment—is*
> *the true measure of lasting greatness.*
> —Billy Graham

Complacency

Often you may get caught up in the comfort of your safe environment. This is secure, predictable, and…mediocre. There is nothing wrong with this. But if you ever want to excel, move forward, grow, or advance, you need to allow yourself to feel some discomfort. Let this be a guide to make some adjustments and try something new. In your business or career, take an additional step or ask for something challenging. Make additional calls. Try something you may have been afraid to try before. Expand your mind, expand your thoughts, strengthen your feelings, then take some action! Ask yourself, what's the worst that can happen? *"Shoot for the moon; even if you miss, you'll land among the stars"* (Les Brown).

Complacency leads to boredom, hinders creativity, and dampens motivation for accomplishment. Underperformance may occur and prevent you from reaching your full potential. You are likely to disengage and lose interest in the possibility of growth and advancement. There is a lack of corroboration and adapting to shifting circumstances. This applies to all aspects of your life. Not only in business but also in your personal life, it is easy to become complacent.

You must continually move forward in your relationships, your faith, learning, and growing. Never stop learning. Push past the fear or discomfort, and focus on growth. Continued learning leads to increased job satisfaction, improved self-esteem, an expanded network of friends and acquaintances, building character, a more colorful life, and increased earning and opportunity potential. You should strive to learn something new each and every day. Set goals and track your progress. Be flexible and willing to make adjustments. Find creative ways to alter your current routine and push past the block in perspective.

It is during the times of your trials and challenges that you grow the most. You don't just go through trials; you grow through trials. Trials are inevitable. You should work to cultivate a positive attitude toward affliction. *"Consider it all joy, my brethren, when you encounter various trials"* (James 1:2 NASB 1995). In other words, your outlook determines your outcome. How you perceive trials will inevitably influence how they impact you. Program your mind so when, not if, trials arrive, your thoughts are already programmed to productively and appropriately work through the situation with endurance, *"knowing that the testing of your faith produces endurance"* (James 1:2 NASB 1995). These challenges are all opportunities for spiritual growth.

Bad attitude

The work ethic today has changed drastically from even a decade ago. I am old-school and believe income should be *result-driven*. Working smart and diligently should prove to be more valuable than someone lazily performing bare-minimum tasks. I do not believe everything should be so as not to offend someone. When you take the time to acquire valuable education and utilize this wisdom for a business endeavor, you deserve a financially equivalent outcome. This is the basis of success and what free enterprise is all about. Regarding being paid based on time from a salary or service-driven business, these forms of income are admirable and respectable. Use a portion to invest in storage rentals, tax liens, or even silver. These are just some examples of potential investment opportunities that could be utilized to grow wealth.

What if you and your attitude are obstacles to your success? Having a bad attitude is a harmful work ethic that must be addressed immediately. You must find the source of this behavior and reframe it with a positive outlook. Focus on a positive mindset. I believe in great effort and performance in all you do, whether it's family or friend relationships, business, home projects, volunteering, raising a family, or listening to someone who is lonely. When you give the best of yourself, the positive energy is disbursed and permeates throughout your immediate environment, often leading to favorable outcomes. Knowledge does lead to power, and power to confidence. Having confidence in what you do also submits positive and productive energy. This opens your mind to more creative and lucrative thoughts and, therefore, a greater likelihood of fruitful results.

A bad attitude is quite often partnered with blame. Usually, if you have a bad attitude, you are quick to blame others for the unfavorable circumstances you are experiencing. Ask yourself what you need to take responsibility for. *You* may be your biggest obstacle to success. Take responsibility for yourself, your actions, and your circumstances. This will undoubtedly enhance your leadership and success potential.

A positive attitude and work ethic will increase the likelihood of achieving favorable outcomes. You will be rewarded as you deliver quality work in a timely manner. You will build a powerful reputation and be noticed for your integrity and commitment to yourself and the company, and will be highly desirable by other businesses or employers. Perform your duties to the best of your ability with dedication and professionalism. You will find you have greater job satisfaction and career advancement when you hold yourself to these high standards and are accountable for all of your actions.

Bitterness

Have you ever had a previously bad experience in the workplace? Maybe a conflict with another employee, or even worse, a wrongful termination? A traumatic effect like this may leave you feeling bitter. I have experienced a situation in the workplace with a jealous boss—twice! My work and commitment were excellent, and I succeeded in everything I did. And that was the problem. They responded unethically, leaving me confused, frustrated, and bitter.

Bitterness is a harmful emotion that can destroy relationships and inhibit creative abilities. The one who remains bitter is the one with the problem. Even while what was done unto you was wrong and beyond your control, this is a negative emotion and can lead to many adverse health concerns if left to fester. Bitterness is all about hate and anger. If this is something that is weighing you down, you must free yourself from this negative state of mind to protect your health, well-being, and relationships.

Think about why you are so bitter. What part did you play in it, if any? There may be a lesson involved that could lead to an opportunity for your growth. Find a motivation to change this thought pattern. Your health, well-being, and relationships are all great reasons to replace this negative emotion. Forgive yourself for allowing this to persist, and as difficult as it may be, forgive the offender.

This is for you. The bitterness does not affect the offender, only you. By forgiving this person, you rid your mind of the negative clutter that is programming it. This will take time. Pray for that person, as he or she must be hurting and miserable inside to have been driven to do the unethical thing that was done unto you. Focus on building new habits and reframing thoughts. Avoid potential triggers and practice positive thoughts and high-frequency energy techniques like mindfulness and meditation. Enjoy nature, and get moving outside to circulate blood flow and positive feel-good hormones. Realize how much negative energy you have expended on allowing this person or situation to live rent-free in your mind.

Actually, it was "rent-negative" as the offender or situation withdrew deposits from you! From this point on, hold yourself accountable for your emotions and control where they wander. Perhaps schedule some relaxing events to look forward to, to distract and redirect your thoughts. As discussed earlier, get your praise on and express gratitude for all of your blessings. Try serving others. It is very difficult to be bitter when focusing on serving someone else in need.

> *If you spend your time hoping someone will*
> *suffer the consequences for what they did*
> *to your heart, then you're allowing them to*
> *hurt you a second time in your mind.*
> —Shannon L. Alder

Regret

Regret is a negative feeling of sorrow or lament experienced as a result of something said, done, or not done. Prevention is the best solution, but that may not always occur. Regret may keep you trapped in the past while ignoring the present. It may even prevent you from taking a new action of some sort. There are many harmful health effects associated with regret. Therefore, it is extremely important to resolve these feelings immediately. Very often, regret leads to some form of self-loathing or critical thoughts about yourself. You may consider denying yourself of something or another form of self-punishment.

This negativity may begin to clutter your mind and monopolize your thoughts. An unmet expectation or disappointment is often a root cause of regret. You are perhaps acting without thinking or not taking advantage of a glowing opportunity. This may lead to feelings of guilt, disappointment, rage, and resentment. It is imperative to address these feelings immediately. Ask yourself what else could have been done or changed to alter the outcome. There is a good chance that it was beyond your control.

If this is the case, you must continually replace the thoughts with realistic ones, reframing the event or situation. Meditate, raise your energy level to a high frequency, and follow the exercise at the end of this chapter. If the focus of the regret was your fault, forgive yourself. Be kind, loving, and understanding, and grow from the knowledge you gained from the situation.

If an apology is in order, pursue it quickly and sincerely. Then, as mentioned, replace and reframe your thoughts and work toward removing the negativity from this unfortunate event and focus on the present, where you can positively impact the world surrounding you. Praise and gratitude are also wonderful ways to take your focus off of you and place it upon someone else.

> *Repent, then, and turn to God, so that*
> *your sins may be wiped out, that times of*
> *refreshing may come from the LORD.*
> —Acts 3:19 NIV

Fear

False events *appearing* real—fear only holds the power you give it. You have the power to own and control your thoughts over fear. It is a choice. Fear is generally an emotion regarding something that has not actually happened. Similar to worry, fear is based on an unestablished event. It is important to recognize this so you can begin to gain control over it. Once you disempower this emotion and overcome this lack of control over your thoughts, you can reclaim your joy and productivity again.

Fear is a general term encompassing a wide range of circumstances, such as pain, failure, loss, rejection, speaking, flying, etc. One method for disengaging this emotion from some of the fears mentioned is to take small steps to desensitize yourself from an event, such as speaking, taking on a new task, or making a new friend. Make yourself aware of your fear, maybe even write it down. Share it with a friend or loved one. Acknowledge the reality that it has not happened and change how you think about it.

Perhaps visualize a positive outcome, meditate, or find ways you are able to relax. Exercise or practice deep breathing. Engage in fun activities, read encouraging books, or even dance or sing. Most of all, pray. Pray that God's amazing grace will give you the strength to run toward your fear with courage. Pray that you have the trust and confidence needed to go through these trials.

> *For God has not given us a spirit of fear and*
> *timidity, but of power, love, and self-discipline*
> —2 Timothy 1:7 NLT

> *I prayed to the LORD, and He answered*
> *me. He freed me from all my fears.*
> —Psalm 34:4 NLT

Now that you have done all you can to resolve the source of the fear, use it to motivate you toward your goals! Push past the barrier, and turn that negative energy into positive and productive energy. Try harder, work longer, and give more. Just transform the energy into a useful and empowering source for your advantage. Intentionally *utilize fear* in a way that is most advantageous to you.

> *Do what is right and do not give way to fear.*
> —1 Peter 3:6 NIV

Perfectionism

Perfectionism is a condition of needing everything to be perfect. We are not perfect beings. As a matter of fact, the Bible makes it clear that we all fall short. Romans 3:23 (NIV) says, *"For all have sinned and fall short of the glory of God."* We are all flawed. So, what a relief to know that you and I do not have to be perfect!

There is nothing wrong with embracing high standards or setting the bar at a stretch above last year's goal, but it is harmful to design such a lofty goal that it is unattainable to the point that it affects you emotionally. Not all goals are attainable, and that should be an acceptable measure. If you know you worked diligently toward the goals, enjoy the accomplishments along the journey. The harmful consequences occur if you cannot look at what has been accomplished and enjoy the results but rather dwell on the fact that the ultimate level has not been attained. This may lead to anger, frustration, feelings of failure or inadequacy, and quite often, procrastination will result.

Consider why you think your work or project needs to be perfect. What is the worst-case scenario if it isn't? There are ways to combat the feeling of needing everything to be perfect. Begin with your thoughts. Bring them to awareness, as mentioned previously. Replace these thoughts with reasons why it's okay to perform "greatly" rather than "perfectly." Forgive yourself for the pressure you placed upon yourself. Be kind and realize that no one else expects you to be perfect. It was only in your mind.

Have grace in your thoughts about your performance and realize you really are amazing and are using the gifts and talents you have been given. Reframe your goals and expectations in a new, more reasonable light. The sun will rise the same way it always has, even if your work isn't perfect.

Another point to be made here is that often, if you are a perfectionist with yourself, you may be a perfectionist in assessing other people, such as employees, coworkers, or even your children. The same information applies. They are also imperfect people and would benefit from your grace and forgiveness of yourself and them. Work mindfully through your thoughts and reprogram your mind with loving, forgiving, and empowering thoughts.

Toxic people

While unfortunate, quite often, there are toxic people in your workplace. Have you ever experienced this? Or perhaps I should ask, have you ever *not* experienced this in a work setting? They may come in the form of harassers, gossipers, bullies, or manipulators. The stress of dealing with toxic people can be harmful to your health, may affect your relationships, and may even hinder your job performance. You cannot fix or change anyone other than yourself, so you must learn how to manage your immediate environment and your response to uncomfortable situations.

Ideas on How to Handle Toxic People in the Workplace:[27]

1. *Find supporters.* Form relationships in your work environment that are positive and job-oriented. There is strength in numbers, so join forces with positive and productive people who align with your work goals. You do not have to work against the toxic person, but rather, counter the effects by focusing on the right things.
2. *Set boundaries.* Rise above the madness of the toxic person and do not respond emotionally. Use

your nonverbal body language to indicate your unwillingness to engage in their manipulation. Avoid toxic situations if at all possible. Know your boundaries, and do not let the offenders penetrate them in any way. Do not drop your standards to their level under any circumstances.

3. *Have good self-care.* You are most susceptible to the toxic effects of others when you are not well-rested or are unhealthy. Meditation may help by keeping your mind off the offending person and on the present moment instead. It calms your brain and gives you more mental clarity. Eat a healthy diet and make sure you are well-nourished. Let your body benefit from healthy choices, which will increase your confidence and help counter the negative effects of your challenging coworker. Take breaks away from this person when possible, and also take advantage of vacation time to escape to a stress-free atmosphere where you can unwind and refresh your mind. Take personal days when you are permitted to do so, and get plenty of rest.

4. *Focus on solutions.* It is pointless to attempt to understand how a toxic person thinks or why they do what they do. This is beyond your control. Focus on what you can control and actions you can take rather than ruminating on what you cannot. Toxic people are driven by nefarious methods and are irrational in their thought processes. You will *never* understand them. They will manipulate at any cost. Think of ways to manage your situation and allow you to feel more in control. And as they are sneaky and manipulative, watch your back and always document your actions if there is a chance the offender could manipulate situations or events. Detach yourself

where possible, yet protect yourself when corroboration is necessary.

If this toxic person begins to dominate your thoughts, and it is apparent your employer is willing to tolerate their continued bad behavior, consider researching other companies that will benefit from your talents and work ethic. Your sanity is more valuable than any one job or position.

Toxic people can invade your personal life as well as your workspace.

Seven Types of Toxic People:[28]

1. *The Conversational Narcissist.* This type of person loves to talk about themselves. It will be difficult to get a word in edgewise. They are completely self-centered and will never be attentive to your needs. They love to talk, think, and care for themselves.
2. *The Strait Jacket.* This type of person strives to control everything and everyone around them. They want to be in charge of what you do, say, and even what you think. They fall apart if you disagree with them and work tirelessly to convince you that they are right. They want you to be in complete alignment with them. They will attempt to gain control of your emotional and mental freedom until you have nothing left.
3. *The Emotional Moocher.* They may also be known as a *"spiritual vampire,"* as they tend to suck the positivity out of you, or bleed you emotionally dry. They always have something sad, negative, or pessimistic to say. They can never see anything positive and will bring you down with them.
4. *The Drama Magnet.* Something is always wrong. And once it is resolved, there is another problem

or two that emerges. They only want your empathy, sympathy, or support, but never your advice. They would rather complain than actually fix the problem. They are victims who thrive in a crisis.

5. *The JJ.* This is a *Jealous-Judgmental* person. Jealous people are incredibly toxic because they have so much self-hate that they cannot be happy for others. The jealousy comes out as judgment, criticism, or gossip. They thrive in putting you down so they feel better about themselves. They also take pleasure in talking behind your back.

6. *The Fibber.* They are liars, fibbers, and deceivers, and they are exhausting. It is impossible to trust this type of person in a relationship. Dishonesty is draining.

7. *The Tank.* A tank crushes everything in its path. They are always right and do not care about the feelings or ideas of others. They constantly put themselves first and are incredibly arrogant; even their opinions are stated as facts. They believe they are the smartest person in the room, so they see every person and conversation as a challenge that must be won. They do not see anyone else as an equal, so they are difficult to have a relationship with.

Avoidance of these people is always the best first option. However, this may not always be possible. In that case, rather than enabling them to get their way, you may *"try respectful disagreement instead. You might say, 'I had a different take on the situation,' and describe what really happened. Stick to the facts, without making accusations."*[29]

This most likely won't be what they want to hear, yet you won't be enabling them, and maybe they will be less likely to engage with you next time as they cannot manipulate you for the reaction they crave. Resist the temptation to complain along with them or to defend yourself against their accusations. Perhaps just respond, *"I'm sorry you feel that way."*

Gain an understanding of what the toxic profiles listed previously look like so you can identify them immediately and arm yourself against the manipulation. Be aware of how they make you feel, and allow yourself to be in control of your own emotions and environment. Do not allow yourself to be drawn into their toxic world. Be prepared to walk away, and do not allow them to leave you with a feeling of guilt. You cannot fix them. You can only control yourself and how you handle and respond to the stimulus. Set boundaries, change your routine, always have an exit strategy, and maybe even gently encourage them to seek help. Meditation will help bring you back to a place of calmness.

> *You cannot change the people around you, but you can change the people you choose to be around.*
> —Unknown Author

> *Don't let negative and toxic people rent space in your head. Raise the rent and kick them out.*
> —Robert Tew

Some of your friends may be a negative influence in your life. As you mature in your spirituality, you may begin to find it wise to choose friends carefully. You may even find it necessary to start letting some unhealthy friendships dwindle. They may speak critically or not align with your goals, morality, or your well-being. Become aware of how you feel when you are in the presence of the people you spend time with. Maybe it's time to become less friendly and more cordial, slowly pulling away from the amount of time spent together. Identify the quality of relationships you want in your life.

What are your values? What are your priorities? Start to align your friendships with your standards, and only pursue relationships that allow you to grow and advance. Prune out people that stunt your personal, professional, or spiritual development.

The righteous should choose his friends carefully,
for the way of the wicked leads them astray.
—Proverbs 12:26 NKJV

A wise man is strong, yes, a man of knowledge
increases strength; for by wise counsel you,
you will wage your own war, and in a
multitude of counselors there is safety.
—Proverbs 24:5 NKJV

As iron sharpens iron, so a man sharpens
the countenance of his friend.
—Proverbs 27:17 NKJV

Do not be unequally yoked together
with unbelievers. For what fellowship
has righteousness with lawlessness?
—2 Corinthians 6:14 NKJV

He who walks with wise men will be wise, but
the companion of fools will be destroyed.
—Proverbs 13:20 NKJV

There is an extremely high value placed on friendships. Make sure all of your friendships are aligned with your own values.

As problems are always a part of life, including in the workforce, it is imperative to understand how best to perceive and respond to them. More often than not, there is more than one way to resolve unfavorable or challenging circumstances. I have found that being able to describe/define the problem, then brainstorm best and worst-case scenarios is often helpful. From there, I think about or write down as many different possible solutions that come to mind. Sometimes discussing with a trusted friend or work peer helps give a proper perspective. And, of course, lots of rest and sleep time always provide clarity, as the body works best when not under duress. I am amazed at the new perspective a morning may bring.

Once all of these steps are carried out, the issue has suddenly dwindled, just as my options for resolutions and ability for deductive reasoning have expanded.

There are many, many obstacles that challenge your progress toward becoming successful. These are the same obstacles that are capable of affecting any aspect of your life. Knowing how to cope with them now will help minimize their ugly effects no matter where they creep in. This chapter introduced you to some of the most common and crippling obstacles and ways to deflate their impact. By utilizing the suggestions and practicing the exercises, you will become more efficient in overcoming each of the obstacles listed, plus the same methods may also be useful in other obstacles not listed that may come into play. You are well equipped to dissolve them all.

Prayer

> *Father, I have come to a trying time in my life, and I am not sure which direction to go. I know that if I seek first the kingdom of God and His righteousness, then I will be walking in Your best way for my life, forever and always. Help me LORD to be wise in the decisions I make at this junction, where various doors have seemed to close behind me. Lead me, LORD, in the direction that You would have me go day in and day out. LORD, I want my life to count, and I want to be successful in making a difference. Take my life, LORD, and at this crossroads I ask that You rearrange my direction as best seems to You.*[30]

> *God of all Comfort, I am seeking tranquility for my mind. As I pray and meditate upon Your Word, my mind often drifts to my to-do lists and needs. I pause now from my day. I breathe out a deep sigh from within my soul and ask, will You please quiet my storm? Help me remember all Your*

*goodness to me. Deliver me from anxiety and the
battle that rages for control of my mind. Amen.*[31]

Exercise

Close your eyes and focus on your breathing. Feel your heart
and mind come together in sync. Focus on words such as love and
light in your mind and heart. Repeat words of this kind, such as *Jesus,
love, light,* and *angels* "Fill my energy with love. Fill me with light."
Imagine an aura of light surrounding you, growing brighter and
brighter. Choose every thought carefully and only select high-energy,
high-vibration light thoughts. Choose peace, joy, serenity, calmness,
and self-control.

Feel the light energy expand around you. Let it flood your
heart, mind, and entire body with positive high-frequency energy,
and let it flow into your surroundings. If a negative thought comes
to mind, let it flow through you, but do not let it attach to anything.
Refocus on positive, loving things and visualize the bright light and
powerfully positive energy surrounding you and lifting you up.

Reflection

1. Identify three obstacles to your success. What will you do
    to dissolve them?
2. Which obstacle is the most difficult one to overcome? How
    can you prepare for any future occurrence of this particular
    obstacle?
3. Identify some methods you will utilize to prevent a future
    impact of these obstacles.

Wisdom from the Word

> *Let all bitterness and wrath and anger
> and clamor and slander be put away
> from you, along with all malice*
> —Ephesians 4:31 ESV

*See to it that no one comes short of the grace
of God; that no root of bitterness springing up
causes trouble, and by it many be defiled.*
—Hebrews 12:15 NASB

*So do not fear, for I am with you; do not
be dismayed, for I am your God. I will
strengthen you and help you; I will uphold
you with my righteous right hand.*
—Isaiah 41:10 NIV

CHAPTER 6

Thoughtfully Reprogrammed

Honest awareness

The first step to reprogramming your mind is to know what you are reprogramming. It is imperative to know the problem before you attempt a solution. Take time to observe where your thoughts currently are and where the baseline rests. Are they mostly positive thoughts? Or mostly negative thoughts? Or are they an evenly balanced combination of both?

Remove any blind spots and become honestly aware of your thoughts. In your workplace, how would the most critical person describe your attributes? How would your closest friend describe them? Are you quick to anger? Do you display knee-jerk reactions? Expose them all. Write down your thoughts about your thoughts, and come to the realization of their current status.

If you have taken the time to do this, the most difficult part is completed. Honest and complete self-awareness is *crucial* in this process. And this is a *process*. Reprogramming your mind is not a quick endeavor. Imagine all of the years it took to program your mind to its current condition!

The next step is to determine the type of programming you want your mind to encompass. Would you like your thoughts to be instinctively empowering? Would you like to be slow to anger and have thought-filled responses? You have some work to do. And you have a wonderful start by already identifying the current status of your thoughts and determining where you want them to be.

> *Awareness allows us to get outside of*
> *our mind and observe it in action.*
> —Dan Brule

> *Awareness precedes change.*
> —Robin Sharma

A new perspective

It is easy to become overwhelmed when problems arise. And they always will. How you handle problems is the key to remaining peaceful, joy-filled, and in control. As previously mentioned, when personal problems arise, break them down and examine the possible causes and solutions. It is helpful to have close friends or family to share them with if the issue needs other perspectives. Breaking down the issues and thinking of the right thing to do for the best outcome often minimizes the negative impact of the issue at hand. And I have noticed that writing down steps to take to resolve the issue if it is a complex problem, makes it much more manageable. If a resolution is needed step by step, the process of making a list and checking it off keeps focus on tasks and productivity rather than worry and stress. And positively charged energy will drive you toward the possibility of many potential and successful resolutions.

By changing your perspective, you are able to gain new insights and see things from a different point-of-view and perhaps reach a better understanding. This could result in a more peaceful outcome, inspired creativity, and strengthened relationships. This empowers you to change how you feel about something or someone. If you only see things from one vantage point, you may miss out on a valuable way to experience your life. Your perspective on how you view things is a choice. How wonderful it is that you have control over this aspect. You may alter your view of the world.

For example, you have the choice to control your thoughts and select positive and productive ones and experience your life in a way that supports your goals.

*The moment that you accept life and
your life as it is, is the moment that
you will start to change your life.*
—Rasheed Ogunlaru

*He who asks a question is a fool for a minute;
he who does not remains a fool forever. When
you realize that by changing your perspective,
the big things can be seen as little things, it
becomes much harder to worry about anything.
Commitment is an act, not a word.*
—Jean-Paul Sartre

"By changing perspective to look at an apparently negative situation in a different way, we can imagine a more positive story—one that's more likely to lead to greater happiness."[32]

When we change perspective, not only are we altering our viewpoint, but we are also gaining new insights. It is a healthy way to display more empathy from the vantage point of another. Or gain more compassion. You may even come to the realization that there is a better, quicker, or easier way of doing something you previously did not consider. A new perspective is literally *mind-altering*. It can cause profound changes in your brain. It is a process of moving away from being self-centered to feeling and exhibiting compassion toward *others.*

"If your focus is on something that you perceive to be negative in your life and you come at it from a different angle, then you can feel better about it."[32] This is called *reframing*. This is a positive way to benefit from changing your perspective. Reframing can even be applied to your past by changing the perspective of how you previously viewed an event. This, in turn, could positively impact your present state.

So, we fix our eyes not on what is seen,
but on what is unseen. For what is seen is
temporary, but what is unseen is eternal.
—2 Corinthians 4:18 BSB

Nine Benefits of Receiving a Fresh Perspective:[33]

1. *Become more objective.* It is easy to create an echo chamber if you listen to the same thing or see things from the same point of view. Changing perspective brings you closer to objectivity.
2. *Reassess your point of view.* Someone challenging your belief can open you up to new possibilities by reassessing your perspective. You may form new and more efficient ideas or ways of doing things.
3. *Break old habits.* Your current way of doing things may not be optimal. A fresh perspective may have a big payoff.
4. *Benefit from experience.* Experience from outside of your niche may bring about creative solutions. New ideas may be refreshing and innovative.
5. *Develop flexibility.* It is difficult to take advantage of new opportunities when you are rigid. Stepping out of your comfort zone allows other doors to open.
6. *Create leaders.* Engaging other employees in their opinions may reveal new leaders and talent that had been hidden. Utilize all the potential you can.
7. *Focus on what matters.* Taking a step back and letting others express their thoughts may shine a new light and reveal new things. Perhaps something crucial was being neglected.
8. *Reach new audiences.* Be aware of new audience potential.

9. *Expand into foreign markets.* Collaborating with professionals from diverse backgrounds can resonate new ideas and help avoid misunderstandings.

Personality: strengths and weaknesses

It is wise to take time to identify who you are and reveal your strengths and your weaknesses. Knowing your personality is a key to uncovering your unique self. One method of doing this is by taking a personality test. While there are many to choose from, I have chosen 16personalities.com. This test will identify your strengths and weaknesses and help you understand yourself better. You will be amazed at how your personality can be clearly assessed, perhaps better than you could even define yourself. It can also help you understand other people in your environment, such as family or even work associates.

As the name suggests, sixteen personality types are identified:[34]

Analysts

1. *Architect*: INTJ-A/INTJ-T—imaginative and strategic thinkers with a plan for everything.
2. *Logician*: INTP-A/INTP-T—innovative inventors with an unquenchable thirst for knowledge.
3. *Commander*: ENTJ-A/ENTJ-T—bold, imaginative, and strong-willed leaders, always finding a way or making one.
4. *Debater*: ENTP-A/ENTP-T—smart and curious thinkers who cannot resist an intellectual challenge.

Diplomats

1. *Advocate*: INFJ-A/INFJ-T—quiet and mystical, yet very inspiring and tireless idealists.
2. *Mediator*: INFP-A/INFP-T—poetic, kind, and altruistic people, always eager to help a good cause.
3. *Protagonist*: ENFJ-A/ENFJ-T—charismatic and inspiring leaders who are able to mesmerize their listeners.

4. *Campaigner*: ENFP-A/ENFP-T—enthusiastic, creative, and sociable free spirits who can always find a reason to smile.

Sentinels

1. *Logistician*: ISTJ-A/ISTJ-T—practical and fact-minded individuals whose reliability cannot be doubted.
2. *Defender*: ISFJ-A/ISFJ-T—very dedicated and warm protectors, always ready to defend their loved ones.
3. *Executive*: ESTJ-A/ESTJ-T—excellent administrators, unsurpassed at managing things or people.
4. *Consul:* ESFJ-A/ESFJ-T—extraordinarily caring, social, and popular people, always eager to help.

Explorers

1. *Virtuoso*: ISTP-A/ISTP-T—bold and practical experimenters, masters of all kinds of tools.
2. *Adventurer*: ISFP-A/ISFP-T—flexible and charming artists, always ready to explore and experience something new.
3. *Entrepreneur*: ESTP-A/ESTP-T—smart, energetic, and very perceptive people who truly enjoy living on the edge.
4. *Entertainer:* ESFP-A/ESFP-T—spontaneous, energetic, and enthusiastic people; life is never boring around them.

Knowing your strengths and weaknesses has many advantages. Regarding your strengths, this knowledge allows you to capitalize on your gifts and even enhance and utilize them to your full potential. You can identify what areas you excel in and what would be best to focus on. Knowing your weaknesses is just as important. This reveals where interference may occur and either areas to focus on for improvement or areas to be aware of and avoid to prevent an unfavorable outcome. Knowing this information can help minimize the negative impact that could affect your life.

With more awareness of yourself, you are better able to understand your emotions and how they stem from the programming of your mind. Every step you take to understand better who you are enables you to gain more control of your thoughts, feelings, actions, and reactions. This will help you realize you are in control of your behavior and clarify how you respond to situations.

Personality identification is also useful in helping you recognize how you communicate, lead, negotiate, and corroborate with others and even manage stress. Since communication is key to success in any dimension, it is imperative to understand your best method of communication and how you are most effective in relating to others, especially in a business respect. It is reassuring to know that communication is a skill, and there are many ways communication can be approved upon with courses, coaching, dedication, and more.

Awareness of your personality also helps you identify your method of decision-making and problem-solving. This understanding provides a distinct advantage and more self-confidence when conflict resolution is necessary. You will be better prepared to remain resilient, know your tendencies, and can construct sound plans, even when challenges are substantial. Your ability to resolve problems will be more balanced and effective.

Meditation

Meditation is virtually essential in the process of reprogramming your mind. It allows your conscious mind to rest. Supplying your mind with uplifting thoughts, keywords, or declarations while in a relaxed and elevated state allows them to penetrate more deeply into your subconscious mind without the typical opposition. Guided meditation especially allows for this process as the words are heard verbally from an outside source, providing empowering thoughts into your mind. Your mind is free from choosing words and is open and available to absorb them. Do not overlook the importance of taking time at the end of each chapter to practice the meditation exercise presented. The more you perform this exercise, the easier and quicker you will begin to release the tension and noise around you and transform your energy level to a higher and more beneficial frequency.

Responsibility

You are responsible for yourself and your own success. *"Making excuses for failures or choices in life, instead of taking 100% responsibility for your actions, your thoughts and your goals are classic symptoms of people who fail to succeed, both in their professional lives and personal lives."*[35] Responsibility is taking ownership of how your choices influence your outcomes. When you take responsibility, you learn to manage your time, expectations, your employees if you are in charge, your immediate surroundings, your decisions, and, therefore, your outcomes. It automatically builds your character.

Being responsible means not letting yourself become overwhelmed or take on too many tasks. This would divide your time, thereby decreasing productivity and the quality of your work. This would also lead to a high degree of stress and anxiety. Rather, you take initiative and tackle projects immediately, ensuring no time is squandered senselessly. You give your best for each task you perform, and rather than excuses for challenges that occur, you discover solutions and problem-solving techniques. You are willing to objectively look at the outcomes resulting from your choices, behaviors, and actions, and own each one of them.

"Taking responsibility for your life is taking charge of your life and becoming the main character," rather than being a victim of circumstance.[36] You have the ability to create your own circumstances and how you will respond to the situations you encounter. Blaming others is something that should never occur and is not even considered by a successful person. Taking responsibility becomes a key expression of independence. What matters is your attitude, which you have the authority to choose, as well as your thoughts, behaviors, and feelings. Not only take responsibility but take complete and *deliberate* responsibility with authority in everything you do.

It's only when you take responsibility for your life
that you discover how powerful you really are.
—Allanah Hunt

In the long run, we shape our lives, and
we shape ourselves. The process never ends
until we die. And the choices we make
are ultimately our own responsibility.
—Eleanor Roosevelt

Accountability

Successful people are accountable to someone, even if it's a chosen accountability partner, such as a friend or coworker. Being accountable to someone is a method that acts as a type of conscience and positively impacts both professional and personal development. Knowing you are accountable to someone else, you will find you feel inspired to work more diligently, efficiently, carefully, committedly, and even honestly. There is less room for wavering temptation or procrastination.

In addition, an accountability partner could serve as a guide or mentor to run ideas by for a second opinion or critique your production and help eliminate errors or inconsistencies. Even as a child, it was well known that when someone else was watching you, you tried harder, worked longer, extended yourself more, increased your abilities, expanded your effort, and followed through more often than when you were alone. And when paired up with an accountability partner, you are never alone. The comradery with a like-minded friend or group of friends creates contentment, confidence, and raises your energy level, providing both physical and mental health benefits, and even providing a means of personal and professional growth.

A body of men holding themselves accountable
to nobody ought not to be trusted by anybody.
—Thomas Paine

*You can't talk about leadership without talking
about responsibility and accountability…
you can't separate the two. A leader must
delegate responsibility and provide the
freedom to make decisions, and then be
held accountable for the results.*
—Buck Rodgers

*No individual can achieve worthy goals without
accepting accountability for his or her own actions.*
—Dan Miller

Be intentional

Being intentional means committing to *"living a more present
life aligned with your core values."*[37] It is a lifestyle based on your values and priorities.

Some benefits of being intentional are as follows:

- *You are more present.*
- *You have healthier and happier relationships.*
- *You are aligned with your values.*
- *You create healthy boundaries.*
- *You communicate more confidently.*
- *You create better emotional and mental health.*
- *You have better physical health.*

Being intentional goes hand-in-hand with being responsible
and accountable. You become more aware of how you speak to others and treat them. You are more aware of how you communicate
with others, positively affecting your relationships. You are able to
say no when appropriate and can identify relationships or situations
that drain your energy. You live a more peaceful life because the
decisions you make align with your values, and you are better able
to accept the outcomes of situations knowing this. When you start

living intentionally, you stop blaming others and reacting defensively and begin to take control of what you can and let go of what you cannot control.

> *Live less out of habit, and more out of intent.*
> —Anonymous

> *Intentional living is the art of making our*
> *own choices before others' choices make us.*
> —Richie Norton

Neuroplasticity

"Neuroplasticity is the brain's capacity to continue growing and evolving in response to life experiences. Plasticity is the capacity to be shaped, molded, or altered; neuroplasticity, then, is the ability for the brain to adapt or change over time, by creating new neurons and building new networks."[38]

This all means that it is possible to change a pattern of thinking and develop a new mindset, memories, or skills. The brain can be rewired. You do not have to be stuck in an unhealthy way of thinking. Your brain is resilient, and lifelong stimulation, in moderation, is necessary for optimal brain health and to keep it evolving. Physical activity is a powerful way to open up the "windows of plasticity." *"It stimulates the release of the substance known as brain-derived neurotropic factor (BDNF), which sets in motion the growth of new synaptic connections and bolsters the strength of signals transmitted from neuron to neuron."*[38]

Therefore, even walking for an hour a day at least five days of a week increases brain matter, thus improving learning and memory. What does all of this mean? Start moving! Start walking daily, do some form of activity, dance, mow the lawn, park at the far end of the parking lot, and walk further than usual. Make a habit of moving more. Lift some light weights. Get the heart pumping and blood flowing. Release positive energy into the synapses of your brain. Take a moment to see how in a YouTube video, Sven Otten integrates dancing into all aspects of his life—in a mall, on an escalator, in a bank, at a fruit stand, in the streets, through a parking lot, and even in the bathroom (https://www.youtube.com/watch?v=wNJ-hBA_-80)!

Break bad habits

Breaking a bad habit requires change. It requires stepping outside of your comfort zone and may even be slightly intimidating. You will need to be persistent and determined in order to overcome the ingrained nature of this undesirable behavior. *"Breaking bad habits is a far more complicated process than making new ones."*[39]

Here are a few suggestions on how to overcome an unwanted habit:

1. *Make the habit hard to do.* Find a way to make this undesirable activity harder to accomplish so it becomes less tempting to do. Make it inconvenient and unappealing.
2. *Design the bad habit out of your life.*
3. *Replace the bad habit with a good one.* Find activities or options that are even more enjoyable, productive, and more aligned with your values and beliefs. Go for a walk and get some fresh air. Enjoy nature.
4. *Find an accountability partner.* Encourage each other in support of replacing your bad habit with a good one.
5. *Help or serve someone else.* Engaging time or conversation with another person, especially if they have a need you can meet, helps remove the focus off of the habit and onto someone else. And ultimately, the positive energy feeling that arises from helping others cannot be surpassed.
6. *Be consistent.* Repetition is necessary not only to break a bad habit but also to build a new and healthier one.
7. *Be patient.* Breaking a habit takes a great deal of time and effort. In addition, you may encounter setbacks or delays. Show yourself some grace during these challenging times. Remain motivated to rid yourself of the habit, knowing

you are gaining control of an area of your life that has been previously bound.

8. *Be deliberate and determined.* Clearly identify your goal and plan out steps on how to achieve it. Writing this plan down will increase the likelihood of its occurrence.

9. *Meditate.* Clear your mind and raise your vibrations to high-frequency levels.

10. *Pray.* Prayer is a powerful way to place your trust in the one who makes everything possible.

11. *Reward yourself.* Celebrate each milestone of self-improvement. Each step along the way builds upon the continual journey of success. Positive reinforcement will subconsciously allow your brain to focus more attention and positive energy on the choices which align with your value system.

By following the previous steps and being intentional in the process, it is possible to eliminate nearly all of the bad habits in your life.

Affirmations versus declarations

While a positive affirmation is a way to focus on most likely a favorable occurrence, your mind is keen enough to know that this statement is not actually true at the moment. It is about a possible future event. There is no doubt there are numerous benefits to affirmations, such as an elevated energy level and perhaps motivation or a sense of serenity and calmness. However, there is no ownership of an affirmation. You are simply affirming a nonexistent event. With a declaration, on the other hand, there is a clear delineation of ownership. *"To affirm means to 'state positively, confirm.' To declare means to 'make known officially, formally, to make it evident.'"*[40]

When you declare something, you are owning it now, at this present moment. In the "vibrational world," you exhibit resistance to statements that have not yet occurred in the present. This then serves as an obstacle in the process you are attempting to achieve through an affirmation. On the other hand, when you "declare" something both internally and out loud, you are stating that you already are this thing you are declaring. And this is something the vibrational world is able to align with.

As you think the thoughts of the person making the declaration, your speech will align with your thoughts. Learn to be more aware of your self-talk and think before you speak. How do you want the self-talk to align with your intentions? Let your declarations align your thoughts and your words, and choose them carefully. They will ultimately affect your actions.

> *If you believe, you will receive*
> *whatever you ask for in prayer.*
> —Matthew 21:22 NIV

> *He who trusts in himself is a fool, but one*
> *who walks in wisdom will be safe.*
> —Proverbs 28:26 BSB

Set boundaries

Boundaries are guidelines that you establish. It is very important to set clear boundaries in your business or workplace. This will help to eliminate many potential issues, prevent you from being taken advantage of, and may even allow you to be more effective in all you do.

Sometimes, when you are a new employee or just starting a business, it is easy to be zealous and perhaps have an inclination to overdeliver. It is admirable to be energized and ambitious, and it is always advantageous to give your best in your performance. However, if you give too much, you risk fatigue or burnout, may become careless or sloppy in your performance, and potentially may build resentment.

Whether as an employee or a business owner, it's up to you to set your own boundaries. Boundaries vary widely, and some include contact, time, service, task, alignment, and personal boundaries. As you enforce your established perimeter, you become more confident, and the confines become more comfortable, possibly even developing into a habit. Established boundaries provide for a clear way to communicate your expectations. Having them will help eliminate misunderstandings and confusion. By setting business boundaries, you are able to have the best of both worlds—your business and personal life.

Define your objectives and use them as a guide for your boundaries. Do not allow anything to occur intentionally outside of these objectives. You may even consider implementing policies to help better establish your guidelines.

Seven Unexpected Benefits of Setting Boundaries at Work:[41]

1. *You are able to express your expertise.* Your confidence will grow as your expertise becomes well-defined, and others will know what to expect from you.

2. *You can create order and better manage chaos.* Boundaries provide the necessary structure to help avoid chaos and regulate demands and activities.

3. *You can guard your energy against negativity.* Firm boundaries let in what you want and keep out what you do not want.

4. *You can create greater alignment and productivity.* Clear boundaries are built upon your values, purpose, and mission. When you are clear about them, it's easier to attract ideal relationships, clients, and opportunities that are aligned.

5. *You will be able to lead effectively.* With your boundaries based on your core values, it is clear what your integrity will allow you to do and to avoid. It lays the groundwork for building trust and dependability.
6. *You can guard against the manipulation of others.* It's far more difficult to be preyed upon by manipulative or narcissistic personalities. You are able to say no with grace and grit.
7. *You are better able to protect personal assets.* Clear boundaries help safeguard your time, talent, skills, and abilities.

Review your boundaries periodically, and make adjustments where necessary to make sure they remain relevant. Boundaries are essential in business to protect yourself from overextension, build long-term relationships, and grow a healthy business.

'No' is a complete sentence.
—Annie Lamott

The difference between successful people and really successful people is that really successful people say 'No' to almost everything.
—Warren Buffet

Compassionate people ask for what they need. They say no when they need to, and when they say yes, they mean it. They're compassionate because their boundaries keep them out of resentment.
—Brene Brown

The type of person you are is usually reflected in your business. To improve your business, first improve yourself.
—Idowu Kovenikan

Establishing personal boundaries is essential to your health as well as the health of your relationships. They allow you to determine how you want to be treated and what you are willing to tolerate. You are able to design a framework within your environment and how you accept the world around you. Many people do not understand what boundaries are. You are responsible for establishing and making known to them what you will or will not endure. It is not always evident when a boundary is being crossed. However, you may find yourself feeling uncomfortable in a given situation.

Trust your intuition, and take control of your immediate environment. This may very well bring the present occurrence back to a healthy relationship with a clear understanding of how you want to be treated. Unfortunately, in our culture, narcissists are notorious for violating boundaries. They are self-absorbed and feel entitled to your space. There are many other toxic people that have the potential to affect your boundaries. Make yourself aware of these people who are inclined to manipulate you and violate your boundaries. Be assertive and stand your ground.

Without clear boundaries, you may lose respect for yourself as well as the respect of others. There may be a loss of control of your business or the direction of it or your life. There will most likely be increasing distractions and the likelihood of falling short of goals, leading to guilt, anxiety, or even depression. This would result in losing interest or passion for your business, career, or life in general.

> *When you notice someone does something toxic for*
> *the first time, don't wait for a second time before*
> *you address it or cut them off. Many survivors*
> *are used to the 'wait and see' tactic which only*
> *leaves them vulnerable to a second attack. As*
> *your boundaries get stronger, the wait time gets*
> *shorter. You never have to justify your intuition.*
> —Shahida Arabi

> *Lack of boundaries invites lack of respect.*
> —Anonymous

*Boundaries define us. They define what is me
and what is not me. A boundary shows me where
I end and someone else begins, leading me to a
sense of ownership. Knowing what I am to own
and take responsibility for gives me freedom.*
—Henry Cloud

*Your personal boundaries protect the inner core
of your identity and your right to choices.*
—Gerard Manley Hopkins

*Boundaries are part of self-care. They
are healthy, normal, and necessary.*
—Doreen Virtue

Think bigger

Regret is an unfavorable feeling which can be destructive and self-defeating. Regret can be prevented. It's okay to think bigger than what is being offered. It may take reprogramming the mind to instinctively think bigger when it comes to business and growth. An old but effective cliché: is your glass half empty or half full? Positive thinking often starts with self-talk. If your thoughts are positive, you will have an optimistic approach to responding to your business interactions. Strong motivation for asking for more will improve your chances of hearing a yes in response to your requests. Challenging your thinking by considering why you feel or react a certain way can give birth to new ideas, expand your thinking, and create new and energized feelings leading to lucrative and prolific results.

By now, you have identified some or many obstacles that may have been impinging your progress. Hopefully, you took some time to resolve the obstacles and clear your mind to rebuild yourself more successfully than ever before. Now it is time to establish a *vision*. Make it a *big* vision. Visions and values cannot help but intersect when you design a successful blueprint for any type of venue, whether professional, personal, or spiritual.

Steps to Establish a Vision Into a Reality:[42]

1. *Establish a clear direction.* A distant reference point often makes a path straighter. This will bring clarity and eliminate confusion.

2. *Focus your attention.* Focus is necessary so lower priorities do not steal time and energy from the central vision. It will eliminate distractions. If your vision becomes deeply planted within your subconscious mind, your thoughts and responses will become proactive rather than reactive.

3. *Articulate values.* Make sure your *values* are clearly known. Basic positive and productive values include integrity, honesty, hard work, and fairness, to name a few.

4. *Enlist others to help with implementation.* According to John Kotter, *"No one individual, even a monarch-like CEO, is ever able to develop the right vision, communicate it to large numbers of people, eliminate all the key obstacles, generate short-term wins, lead and manage dozens of change projects, and anchor new approaches deep in the organization's culture. Weak committees are even worse. A strong guiding coalition is always needed—one with the right composition, level of trust, and shared objectives. Building such a team is always an essential part of the early stages of any effort to restructure, reengineer, or retool a set of strategies (or, we may add, move a vision to reality.)"*

5. *Communication.* Use all forms of communication possible to get the word out.

6. *Empower followers.* Encourage collaboration with others and develop a supportive environment. Engage others who have different strengths, tal-

ents, and abilities. Allow them to embrace some
responsibility in bringing the vision to fruition.

Let your values be your platform for your vision. They will continue to communicate to others who you are and serve as a reminder
to you as well. You will need a strong sense of determination and commitment to set your vision in motion and pursue it. Your vision will
set the direction and purpose of whatever it is you are establishing.

This chapter is rich with empowering values to build into your
mind, replacing the obstacles from the previous chapter and programming your mind with new and automatic responses when called
upon for action, starting with awareness. Identify your personality
type and define your strengths and weaknesses. Build up and capitalize on your strengths and account for your weaknesses, whether
by working to improve them or strategically not allowing them to
interfere. Be intentional, responsible, and accountable in all of your
interactions, professionally, personally, and spiritually.

Take the time to slowly read through each of the reprogramming values, practice the suggested exercises, and create new "good"
habits with these phenomenal characteristics. Practice them daily
and internalize them. Perform the meditation, and be intentional in
soaking in each of these qualities of true leaders. Consistently think
bigger and set clearly defined boundaries. You are responsible for
your own success, and you are well-equipped with the right tools to
be abundantly successful.

Do not conform to the pattern of this world, but
be transformed by the renewing of your mind.
Then you will be able to test and approve what
God's will is—His good, pleasing and perfect will.
—Romans 12:2 NIV

Prayer

Heavenly Father, today I surrender my thoughts and mind to You. Help me retrain my thoughts so that they are in line with Your will for my life. I choose to have a positive attitude of faith and expectancy as I develop new skills and seek to reprogram my mind. Teach me to be intentional and set clear boundaries based on my values, and ultimately, Your values. Provide me with the strength to take responsibility for all of my actions and hold me accountable for each decision I make. Guide me always to be open to new perspectives and grant me discernment in the process. Thank You for empowering me to enjoy this life You have for me. In Jesus's name. Amen.

Exercise

Close your eyes and focus on your breathing. Feel your heart and mind come together in sync. Focus on words such as love and light in your mind and heart. Repeat words of this kind, such as *Jesus, love, light,* and *angels.* "Fill my energy with love. Fill me with light." Imagine an aura of light surrounding you, growing brighter and brighter. Choose every thought carefully and only select high-energy, high-vibration light thoughts. Choose peace, joy, serenity, calmness, and self-control.

Feel the light energy expand around you. Let it flood your heart, mind, and entire body with positive high-frequency energy, and let it flow into your surroundings. If a negative thought comes to mind, let it flow through you, but do not let it attach to anything. Refocus on positive, loving things, and visualize the bright light and powerfully positive energy surrounding you and lifting you up.

Reflection

1. Think of a time when you did not take responsibility for your actions. Think of how you could better respond to that situation.

2. Who is your accountability partner? If you do not have one, choose someone you will ask to hold you accountable. It could be for work, exercise, finances, etc.
3. Think of one to three people you need to establish boundaries for. Are there any you should break away from permanently? Are there any boundaries you should set for your work environment?

Wisdom from the Word

> *So then, each of us will give an*
> *account of ourselves to God.*
> > —Romans 14:12 NIV

> *Do not be deceived: 'Bad company*
> *ruins good morals.'*
> > —1 Corinthians 15:33 ESV

> *Keep this Book of the Law always on your*
> *lips; meditate on it day and night, so that you*
> *may be careful to do everything written in it.*
> *Then you will be prosperous and successful.*
> > —Joshua 1:8 NIV

CHAPTER 7

Masterfully Conditioned

Listening

"*The majority of failures in the workplace and in relationships are due to people's inability to listen.*"[43] Often, hearing is mistaken for listening. While hearing is a physical process, listening is an intellectual activity that is more extensive. It involves processing and understanding the information as well. There is no better way to find out what the wants and needs of others are, except by listening. You will know exactly what people want rather than guessing or assuming.

Listening allows you to see into the hearts and minds of your business associates. Successful people know the value and importance of listening. It is the basis of good, open, and honest communication.

There are many obstacles to listening. Sometimes you may be thinking about the answer you want to hear and not quite paying attention to their actual answer. Or you may be formulating what you want to say next and fail to listen to what was actually said. This is often the case when an introduction is made. Think about how often you do not remember the person's name you were just introduced to only seconds ago. Maybe it is an issue of focus. You have so much on your mind that the distractions prevent you from concentrating on the conversation. Or it could be a matter of pride or an ego. Perhaps the recipient of the conversation is someone new, younger, or an amateur with less knowledge and experience.

In business and personal relationships, it is crucial to make becoming an excellent listener a priority. Be aware that the other person also wants to share information that is important to them. I have always been taught to focus on their right eye. Make gentle but consistent eye contact and stay focused on them and what they are saying. You may even interject and repeat some of the things they say, both to help engage you in the conversation as well as send them a message that you are focused on them and what they are conveying to you, especially when it comes to their name.

When introduced, repeat their name out loud, which is a secondary way of helping you remember it from both hearing it from them and saying it from your own mouth. Do not interrupt as they are speaking. Truly care about them and the content of their message. Rather than forecast in your mind any preconceived notions of what they may say, allow their words to deliver the message. Listen with both your head and your heart.

"Listening is both an art and a science."[43]

Here are reasons why listening is a crucial skill for success:

1. *Listening* is a crucial part of being successful, as every idea starts with information, and that information comes from listening.
2. *Listening* is a skill that you can cultivate.
3. *Listening* is the key to knowing what others want, not what you want; it is a little thing that makes a big difference.
4. *Listening* is like planning; it pays off, will save you from making careless mistakes, and can even improve the effectiveness and efficiency of your organization.
5. By *listening*, you will be able to hear what other people don't because the truth is that many people have eyes but do not see and have ears but do not listen. Do not be one of these people.
6. Successful people are good *listeners* because they understand how input from their environment can be critical, crucial, and central to the strategy of their business.

As I have been taught, you have two ears and one mouth. You should spend twice as much time listening as you spend talking.

One of the sincerest forms of respect is actually listening to what another has to say.
—Bryant McGill

Compromise

The best form of negotiation results in a win-win for all people involved. Think of a time when you were working with someone to find a solution, whether in your personal or professional life, and the results heavily favored the other person. How did you feel? I bet you were left feeling somewhat cheated, frustrated, disappointed, maybe violated, and most definitely angry that the results were unbalanced and unfair.

A compromise is about finding common ground or at least a place where you feel like you have gained some things and let go of some things, just as the other person has. The most successful compromises occur when your goal is the priority that both parties are at least reasonably satisfied with the outcome. It's important to understand that the other party involved has needs as well, and by acknowledging the importance of their side of the negotiation, you are more likely to work toward common ground.

There are seven principles summarized by Inc.com that can help allow you to make better compromises in the workplace. Seven Principles for Better Compromise in the Workplace:[44]

1. *Know what's worth compromising.* Think about and determine in advance what is worth it to you.
2. *See compromise as a strength, not a weakness.* Think of a discussion or a debate as a means of both parties getting the most value out of a situation. It is a way of demonstrating your confidence in the fact that a situation can be resolved adequately.

3. *Be transparent with your intentions.* Be direct and let them know if you fundamentally disagree but that you are willing to meet in the middle. This may open the discussion to a meaningful level and proactively demonstrates that you are sincere in your intentions.

4. *Discover your opponents' true needs.* One of your best tools for success is acknowledging and understanding your opponents' real needs. Dig deeper, if necessary, to make sure they are known.

5. *Make multiple suggestions.* When a person has two or more options instead of one, he or she may be more willing to move forward and be happier with the end result. This may open you to more options as well.

6. *Escalate when appropriate.* Sometimes, further effort for a compromise may be necessary, and you may need to escalate your offer, moving the middle ground somewhat closer to your counterpart's relative position. You must determine whether or not it's worth this escalating step.

7. *Know that not all compromise attempts will work.* Go into the potential compromise knowing that there's a chance your efforts won't work at all. Some people are fundamentally unwilling to compromise, and sometimes there really isn't a middle ground between two opposed positions. Do not let this discourage you from trying again in the future.

Independent thinking

Rather than falling into mob mentality, consider throwing aside conformity and seek to understand spiritual themes direct from your own heart rather than through that of someone or something else. *"The fear of the Lord is the beginning of knowledge, but fools despise wisdom and instruction*" (Proverbs 1:7 NIV). Make critical thinking your regular method of thinking, finding your boundaries and values from God alone.

Some characteristics of independent thinkers are as follows:

1. *The ability to ignore.* You will encounter resistance from people who are threatened by your desire to change or not conform. You may choose to ignore them.
2. *The ability to seek the truth.* Empowerment means challenging the borders of comfort—venturing beyond where you normally stop. Change may initially "feel wrong" to old habits. Eventually, it will feel very right and true, but you must travel through doubt and uncertainty to arrive there.
3. *The ability to step aside.* Choose to yield. This is how you can sometimes deal with a difficult and obnoxious person. They relish "the fight" and may become powerless when you consciously let them win. The real empowerment is yours as you refuse to fight.

Independent thinkers do not seek the approval of other people. This saves a tremendous amount of energy. The power that begins to arise from within is breathtaking. Escape the false reality you are living in and *think for yourself.*

> *Responsibility to yourself means refusing to*
> *let others do your thinking, talking, and*
> *naming for you; it means learning to respect*
> *and use your own brains and instincts;*
> *hence, grappling with hard work.*
> —Adrienne Rich

> *Blind belief in authority is the*
> *greatest enemy of truth.*
> —Albert Einstein

Small is the number of them that see with their
own eyes and feel with their own hearts.
—Albert Einstein

And you shall know the truth, and
the truth shall set you free
—John 8:32 NLT

Compliments and the power of receiving

A compliment is a form of powerful and positive encouragement. Even if the words are small, the effect is very large.

Too often we underestimate the power of a touch,
a smile, a kind word, a listening ear, an honest
compliment, or the smallest act of caring, all of
which have the potential to turn a life around.
—Leo Buscaglia

A sincere compliment has the power to put people at ease and transform vibrations into positive energy. Not only does the receiver benefit but also the giver is favorably affected by this kind gesture. Make yourself aware of all of the opportunities available to amplify the energy and light up someone's day. And if you are the receiver of a compliment, be sure to fully accept and receive the generous gift.

Quite often, people are quick to discount a compliment and shy away from accepting this gift. Instead, graciously receive it with a smile and a thank you. There is a positive atmosphere created from a simple compliment with the power to transform your feelings.

I will be generous with my love today. I will
sprinkle compliments and uplifting words
everywhere I go. I will do this knowing
that my words are like seeds and when

they fall on fertile soil, a reflection of those
seeds will grow into something bigger.
—Steve Maraboli

It is not always easy to be the receiver of things; sometimes, it takes deliberate learning how to feel comfortable with receiving. It is easy to become a little too self-reliant. "There is strength in numbers" is an old cliché concluding that the more people present to contribute to a task, the less demand there is for time and energy. Be committed to having what you desire in life. Keep a vision in sight every day of something to move toward. I have found this to be encouraging and provide purpose and motivation in striving toward a goal.

It is wonderful to be independent. However, routinely refusing the help of others may cause a falling away from a relationship. Sometimes accepting help may allow you to feel vulnerable or may lead to feelings of guilt. It is valuable to know that accepting help is not a sign of weakness. It is important to find the source of discomfort causing the resistance. Is it pride? Or maybe guilt? Think about it from the other person's perspective. Not accepting their offer is sending them a message of rejection.

It is okay to let it be a win-win for the giver and the receiver. Even God offers us a free gift, as in Romans 6:23 ESV. *"For the wages of sin is death, but the free gift of God is eternal life in Christ Jesus our Lord."* When complimented, say "Thank you" and mean it. Be grateful for all you currently have, even your challenges. Challenges are opportunities for letting go of negativism and creating new and empowering beliefs. And it is reassuring to know you are not alone.

Contentment and gratitude

Contentment and gratitude are inseparable. The simple discipline of focusing on the good things in your life will undoubtedly lead to gratitude and appreciation. Gratitude helps to reprogram your mind for positivity and seeing the beauty in the world. You are bombarded with so much negativity each day from numerous sources, which diminishes your capacity to feel appreciation readily.

Gratitude is an effective way to train your mind to see goodness throughout the day. Perhaps you could keep a daily journal of people and things you are grateful for to rediscover all of the blessings surrounding you that may be overlooked. Happiness is based solely on your decision to be happy. It is a choice. Yet never become so content that you cannot find room for improvement.

Personally, I have learned to be happy with what I have. *"Godliness with contentment is great gain"* (1 Timothy 6:6 NIV). I am fully content with where I am and all that I have. However, that does not mean it wouldn't be fun or exciting for continued growth in all aspects of my life. In other words, I just cannot be disappointed if I made all the effort possible and tried my best. At that point, I am content with the outcome and am at peace with my efforts. When one door closes, a window or even two may open. There will always be new opportunities.

> *Being content with what you already have*
> *is an art form that leads to a peace that*
> *cannot be replaced by anything else*
> —Elizabeth Gilbert

> *I know what it is to be in need, and I know*
> *what it is to have plenty. I have learned*
> *the secret of being content in any and every*
> *situation, whether well fed or hungry,*
> *whether living in plenty or in want.*
> —Philippians 4:12 NIV

Self-Worth

"Our thoughts, feelings, and behaviors are intimately tied into how we view our worthiness and value as human beings."[45] *"Your self-worth is your evaluation of yourself as a capable and valuable human being deserving of consideration and respect. It is an internal sense of being*

worthy of love." However, the Bible makes it clear how we ought to think and walk.

> *For by the grace given to me I say to everyone*
> *among you not to think of himself more*
> *highly than he ought to think, but to think*
> *with sober judgment, each according to the*
> *measure of faith that God has assigned.*
> —Romans 12:3 ESV

> *So as to walk in a manner worthy of the Lord,*
> *fully pleasing to Him: bearing fruit in every good*
> *work and increasing in the knowledge of God.*
> —Colossians 1:10 ESV

People with positive self-worth tend to have a greater level of self-confidence and self-esteem. Self-worth is affected by thoughts, feelings, emotions, experiences, interactions, beliefs, values, health, etc. Having a positive self-worth can help you set boundaries and is generally paired with a stronger sense of confidence. You are less likely to allow shortcomings to define your identity. You may also be more likely to pursue different opportunities and try new things. Respecting yourself can help gain the respect of others. There are many ways to improve your sense of self-worth, such as engaging in activities you excel in, challenging yourself to strive for more, rewarding yourself when this happens, educating yourself even further in your field or favorite activity, practicing to become better in something, and working on eliminating your negative thoughts and improving the view of yourself.

Empower those around you and build up others. It is difficult to feel low about yourself when you are serving others. Transform the energy surrounding you to a high-frequency level, and allow it to elevate you, and perhaps even positively affect those around you.

We cannot think of being acceptable to others
until we have first proven acceptable to ourselves.
—Malcolm X

As long as you look for someone else to validate
who you are by seeking their approval, you
are setting yourself up for disaster. You have
to be whole and complete in yourself. No one
can give you that. You have to know who
you are—what others say is irrelevant.
—Nic Sheff

Being whole and complete can only come through Christ, as stated in Colossians 2:10 NTL, "*So you also are complete through your union with Christ, who is head over every ruler and authority.*"

Never let yourself be defined by
someone else's opinion.
—Anonymous

To double your net worth, double your
self-worth. Because you will never exceed
the height of your self-image.
—Robin Sharma

Confidence

"*Confidence is built on different things, but overall, it is built on choices and accomplishments that feed your passion, and that make you feel happy and proud of who you are.*"[46] Discovering them is definitely a worthwhile pursuit.

Here are ways to build your confidence:

1. *Accomplish things.* You ultimately feel better about yourself when you accomplish both small and large goals. Establish

daily, weekly, monthly, and yearly goals. You will begin to see even the small daily goals strengthen your confidence "muscles" and invigorate you to set bigger and more ambitious goals. The progress may be incremental, so do not get discouraged as you practice this skill.

2. *Monitor your progress.* It is often difficult to acknowledge an accomplishment if the progress is not being monitored. Monitoring will allow you to gauge and quantify your progress and help you to stay on course, building confidence as you see the progress in real-time.

3. *Do what is right.* Make sure your choices and decisions align with your belief and value systems. This defines your character and builds confidence as you live by the standards you have set.

4. *Be fearless.* Fears will, unfortunately, creep into anything worth doing. Know your ultimate goal and muster your courage and push through the fears. Fear is discussed in the "Thoroughly Challenged" chapter and describes many ways to decrease or even eliminate fears that will inevitably reveal themselves in the most inopportune times. Remind yourself of your determination to accomplish your goals, and that fear is a false feeling of something that has not even occurred.

5. *Exercise.* Energize yourself with some exercise to improve focus and decrease stress. Exercising will also improve cognition plus many other good-feeling health benefits. Consider lifting some light weights or even heavy ones, for that matter. Improving your muscle tone is an instant confidence builder. You can't help but feel better about yourself with a little definition.

6. *"Hear" constructive criticism.* If something you presented or accomplished is met with a critical response, hear what is said, and consider the value of it. Perhaps it will be a valuable eye-opener to an area you could easily improve or enhance. However, if you know what they said is not accurate, be logical and internalize this truth and disregard

their emotional-based comment. Stand behind your work and the belief that what you created has value.

7. *Do as you say.* Show integrity by doing what you say you will do. Subconsciously, your mind will be aligned with your actions, strengthening your self-confidence. It will also gain you the respect of others, which also will build confidence.

8. *Think long-term.* When you know your destination, you are more confident along the way, making choices that align with the future. It provides you with a blueprint to guide you, which builds more confidence in you and each of your decisions. This will also give you peace of mind by laying a solid foundation for long-term goals knowing each short-term challenge or sacrifice is a stepping stone to a bigger goal.

9. *Be resolute.* The further along your journey to success that you travel, and the more goals you begin to achieve, the more critical people will cross your path, feeling the need to judge or challenge you. Understand that this is a weakness in them, generally a feeling of jealousy for what "they" have not accomplished. It is not actually about you, but rather an insecurity in them. Let it be water off a duck's back, knowing that you *expected* people to react to you this way. It is a great sign that you are growing on your mission of success!

10. *Be content.* Be content on your journey and choose your emotions. Choose to be happy. Yet even as challenges come your way, and they will, you can still be content and confident, knowing you have all the tools you need to overcome each of them.

> *Don't listen to negative influences. Believe in*
> *yourself, and show others what you can do.*
> —Marla Runyan

I can do everything through Christ,
who gives me strength.
—Philippians 4:13 NLT

Trustworthiness

If you are considered trustworthy, you are a valuable and reliable person. It means you take responsibility for your actions and are dependable. Trustworthiness can be proven by keeping your word and honoring your commitments. Your word is a promise that you will or will not do something you say, and others know you will follow through on that promise. *"Many people openly admit that their opinion of another individual is largely based on whether or not that individual is able to keep his word."*[47]

In order to develop deep relationships with other like-minded people, you must be reliable and trustworthy with them. Trust is a vital building block in relationships, professionally, personally, and spiritually. Therefore, the lack of trust could lead to the deterioration of any relationship. *"Jesus calls us to trust Him, and to let go of having to control the outcome of every situation. When we do that, we will have joy, even in challenging circumstances."*[48]

This requires a conscious emotional detachment and letting go of the need to control the outcome of every situation. *"Do not worry"* (Matthew 6:25 NIV). Trust is a choice. Being trustworthy is also a choice. You can choose to be a positive, trustworthy force by being reliable, compassionate, honest, confidential, considerate, and intentional. It is a continual trait, not an endpoint, and it takes daily attention and maintenance. If an apology is needed, pursue this immediately before bitter feelings become rooted. Avoid gossip or misleading conversations, or any other kind of deceitful nature. As Mark Twain said, *"If you tell the truth you don't have to remember anything."*

> *People that have trust issues only need to look*
> *in the mirror. There they will meet the one*
> *person that will betray them the most.*
> —Shannon L. Alder

> *When God takes out the trash, don't go*
> *digging back through it. Trust Him.*
> —Amaka Imani Nkosazana

Chapter 7 continues to define more incredible successful qualities that will enhance your business, personal, and spiritual life skills. It is important to be an independent thinker and be able to interpret and decide for yourself rather than conform to a mob mentality. More and more today, people actually become angry if you do not think or feel like they do. Be unique and stand out. Make listening a key trait you are known for, and be flexible enough to compromise without selling yourself short.

A win-win outcome is always the most successful and fruitful kind for a long-term relationship. Be trustworthy, confident, and be persistent in building your self-worth. Continue to memorize and practice the skills and exercises suggested further to develop these characteristics into the programming of your mind. Raise your level of consciousness and envelop all of these traits, just as in the previous chapter. When called to action, with your diligent effort to focus on these qualities, you will become a strong, confident, assertive individual who stands out as a leader in every circumstance you encounter.

Prayer

> *God, sometimes I think about how much of my job is listening to those who are hurting. Sometimes I pray about all those without ears to hear, those who are quick to judge or center themselves or say if they had just... So... I think about how often Jesus just sat and listened, really listened and validated people's pain, and then called them by name. Sometimes I think about how much of the community's job is listening, fiercely listening to those who are unheard, or drowned out or ignored; fiercely listening to those who are hurt, without judgment or an agenda…just listening fiercely to those who have been especially hurt, and then I try to practice that fierce listening, taking to heart the cries of injustice, opening my ears to hear and my heart to be melted. Help me to do my job, I pray. Amen.[49]*

> *Heavenly Father, please bless and protect me at work. Help me to find immediate and lasting peace in the workplace. Please guide me to love others and achieve success in all that I do on my job. Help me to deal with competitive, spiteful, negative people in a way that is kind and loving and not to take their actions personally. Please send a steady flow of work that I can easily accomplish. Please guide my bosses to praise my ideas and implement them and bring me job security and respect. Please bring peace to my life now. In Jesus name. Amen.[7]*

Exercise

Close your eyes and focus on your breathing. Feel your heart and mind come together in sync. Focus on words such as love and light in your mind and heart. Repeat words of this kind, such as *Jesus, love, light,* and *angels.* "Fill my energy with love. Fill me with light." Imagine an aura of light surrounding you, growing brighter and brighter. Choose every thought carefully and only select high-energy, high-vibration light thoughts. Choose peace, joy, serenity, calmness, and self-control.

Feel the light energy expand around you. Let it flood your heart, mind, and entire body with positive high-frequency energy, and let it flow into your surroundings. If a negative thought comes to mind, let it flow through you, but do not let it attach to anything. Refocus on positive, loving things, and visualize the bright light and powerfully positive energy surrounding you and lifting you up.

Reflection

1. Name three ways you can improve your ability to listen.
2. How would you rate your ability to compromise? What can you do to improve it even more?
3. Do you consider yourself an independent thinker? Make yourself aware of where your ideas stem from. How can you apply this and the previous traits to your new success plan?

Wisdom from the Word

> *My dear brothers and sisters, take note of*
> *this: Everyone should be quick to listen,*
> *slow to speak and slow to become angry.*
> —James 1:19 NIV

> *Do not merely listen to the Word, and so*
> *deceive yourselves. Do what it says.*
> —James 1:22 NIV

> *I know what it is to be in need, and I know*
> *what it is to have plenty. I have learned*
> *the secret of being content in any and every*

situation, whether well fed or hungry,
whether living in plenty or in want.
—Philippians 4:12 NIV

For I am confident of this very thing, that
He Who began a good work in you will
perfect it until the day of Christ Jesus.
—Philippians 1:6 NASB 1995

CHAPTER 8

Innovatively Refreshed

Innovative

Innovation refers to a process of finding different ways of doing things that are more advanced, creative, improved, sometimes even a little risky, and hopefully, more effective. At least, that is the intent. This may be seen as a positive or negative factor for a business. "Being innovative" is generally a positive characteristic based on curiosity, new perspectives, and an openness to change. Innovative people are analytical and courageous to be able to embrace change with an optimistic outlook. With the immense competition that exists in the workplace today, being innovative is virtually a necessity. It may elevate your market position and get your business noticed.

Being innovative takes lots of creativity and forward-thinking. You are able to foresee potential issues or opportunities in the future and preplan to accommodate future change. It is an asset to be able to bring fresh and stimulating ideas to the table. Practice brainstorming ideas for different ways of doing things. Perhaps reframe the situation in a few different ways. Creativity can actually be sparked with practice. Seek inspiration from many different sources and settings. It is amazing where you can find inspiration. Share your thoughts in conversations with others. Ideas can lead to more ideas, then even more from there. Different perspectives can trigger new thoughts. Being innovative is a characteristic that is sure to get you noticed.

*The only way to discover the limits of the possible
is to go beyond them into the impossible.*
—Arthur C. Clarke

What is now proved was only once imagined.
—William Blake

*If you want something new, you have
to stop doing something old.*
—Peter F. Drucker

*Innovation is seeing what everybody has seen
and thinking what nobody has thought.*
—Dr. Albert Szent-Gyorgyi

Inspirational

Be an inspiration to someone else. "Inspire a fire" in a colleague, friend, or even an acquaintance. Be a giver, and give generously. Aim to be the most inspiring person they have ever met. Ask questions and discover their wants, needs, and "intrigues." What intrigues them? Look at the atmosphere of your company, workplace, or even your own home. Lead by example and set high goals, demonstrating the courage to act, remaining persistent yet authentic and flexible. Let them rise to their full potential. Show your passion and set the standard to exceptional without making unreasonable demands, remaining open for feedback along the way.

Many of the skills discussed in previous chapters come into play at this time, such as deep and active listening, allowing for a new perspective, and showing empathy as you discover the needs of those you are inspiring. Develop trusting relationships and benefit from the collaboration that transpires as you build an understanding from different viewpoints. Realize this is a creative process of mutual respect in and of itself, and it is an inspiration to everyone involved.

Some characteristics with the power to inspire include courage, passion, creativity, confidence, and your drive and ambition. When you radiate these qualities, people are drawn to you and look to you for guidance, leadership, advice, and even friendship. They will also look at your ability to communicate and the practice of taking responsibility for past, present, and future actions. Your ability to overcome challenges and how you cope under stress will be emulated just as much as how you handle your successes.

Ten Different Ways Anyone Can Inspire Those Around Them:[50]

1. *Build up those around you.* Positive reinforcement and recognition can have a tremendous impact. A little compliment goes a long way. This may even boost their confidence and self-worth.
2. *Be enthusiastic.* Your energy can be a powerful motivator. It can also be contagious to those around you. Be enthusiastic about everything in your life—work, relationships, relaxing activities, etc.
3. *Have integrity.* Be consistent with your values, actions, words, and how you treat others at all times. Let your core beliefs and moral compass always align with your behavior.
4. *Be empathetic.* Showing others that you care about them more than their work output is an important part of being a leader. People should always come first.
5. *Maintain a positive outlook.* Accept reality for what it is while still choosing an optimistic outlook for the future. Staying positive during challenging times in itself is an inspiration, as this can be a difficult thing to do.
6. *Practice gratitude.* Gratitude is a powerful catalyst for change. It is a reminder of everything that nourishes and supports you. Showing gratitude can inspire others to do the same.

7. *Stand your ground.* Stay true to your beliefs, personal values, and ethics. You must be seen as a source of stability, continuity, and safety.

8. *Set clear goals and strive to achieve them.* Do everything in your power to achieve your goals. If they appear to be unreachable, do not change the goal; change the approach to the goal. Try something different, invite others to share a new perspective, and increase your output, but do not give up on the goal. It takes a lot of self-discipline and dedication to achieve your goals.

9. *Have passion.* The fires of passion propel your plans into action. Passion promotes productivity and helps you commit to a shared vision.

10. *Challenge them.* Being challenged can help keep your mind sharp and inspired. Continuously challenging those around you will inspire important skills such as brainstorming and creative thinking.

When working with others, make them a part of the team or process. Talk less and listen more. Acknowledge the input of others, and share in the achievements. Support and celebrate individual successes, and show appreciation for all contributions, no matter how small they may be. And although their efforts may not always be for the betterment of your company or business, also share and recognize their personal accomplishments and successes. Show that you care, lead by example, provide honest, constructive feedback, and reward where appropriate.

Find ways to inspire yourself. Consistently taking action is one of the keys to success. However, taking action also expends a massive amount of energy! Inspired action is one of the most powerful ways to motivate yourself, so you must take some time to recharge your own inspiration. What inspires you? What are the best ways to light your fire to inspire?

Seven Ways to Inspire Yourself:[51]

1. *Be decisive.* Start taking action! The act of making a decision and taking action will build momentum. More on decisiveness is found in Chapter 9.
2. *Act like you mean it.* If you act like you mean it, you'll make better choices, show more confidence, and build energy that lets you spiral up. Be bold, direct, and intentional.
3. *Draw from inspirational words of wisdom.* This helps you to summon your inner strength, ultimately from God, the eternal Source of strength.
4. *Stand on the "shoulders of giants."* No matter what challenges you are up against, somebody else has already been there. Draw from their similar experiences.
5. *Play the favorite scenes in your mind.* Utilize a favorite scene from a movie or event from the past or someone else's life that inspires you. Draw on any of these shining moments and remember the feeling that resulted from it. Use it to fire you up.
6. *Shift to the future.* Sometimes, the past can bring you down. Instead, shift to the future and envision the possibilities. By having a compelling vision, you have something to shoot for.
7. *Connect to your values.* By connecting to your values, you tap into your inner source of power, in God himself. Connect everything you do to your values.

Eventually, you will find yourself at a loss for inspiration at some point in your journey. Finding what works best for you is important to build up this valuable asset. Do things that make you happy, exercise, or even show gratitude. Eliminate any obstacles that may be hindering your inspiration. Set incentives for yourself and avoid procrastination. Join forces with an accountability partner and inspire and motivate each other. Find and do whatever it takes to recharge and re-energize yourself as you prepare for the *massive* action ahead!

The value of quiet time

"We are losing our ability to know who we are and what is important to us. We are creating a global machine in which each of us is a mindless and reflexive cog, relentlessly driven by the speed, noise, and artificial urgency of the wired world."[52]

It is important that you build silence, solitude, and time for deep thought into your schedule at some point throughout your day. During this time, you should disconnect from technology and, as much as possible, sit in silence. While your mind will instinctively continue in its frenzy, with practice and time, you will learn how to calm it down, if even for a fifteen-to-thirty-minute break during your day. You will begin to realize everything around you is just fine while you give yourself some serene time alone.

Constantly being busy is diminishing your ability to focus and concentrate. By taking the time to quiet your mind, you will rejuvenate your thoughts and energy and help declutter your mind, leading to greater creativity. You may also improve your health and cognition by allowing distractions to drift away from your peaceful space. Whether you choose to be alone with your thoughts or engage in no thought at all is up to you.

Quiet time to you may look like nine holes on a beautifully manicured golf course, absorbing the stillness of the thicket and snowy ground with your hunting rifle, or time alone in the presence of your heavenly Father. There is no wrong way to enjoy your quiet time. Take a long bath or shower, pray, read, write, bake, sing, take a nap, or just lie down and think.

Time away from distractions will give you more direction, wisdom, and clarity to finish the obligations of the rest of the day. It will also allow you to refocus on the value of your relationships. You will see your actions more clearly and assess your mistakes as well as opportunities you may be able to pursue. While this distraction-free time provides a state of mind in which it is quiet and at peace, there is still an abundance of energy throughout.

> *We need solitude, because when we're alone,*
> *we're free from obligations, we don't need to put*
> *on a show, and we can hear our own thoughts.*
> —Tamim Ansary

> *Spending time alone in your own company*
> *reinforces your self-worth and is often the number-*
> *one way to replenish your resilience reserves.*
> —Sam Owen

> *Be still, and know that I am God.*
> —Lao Tzu

Value of social time

While spending some quiet time alone is healthy, it is also important to spend time socializing with other people, especially friends and family. Being around loved ones is comforting and can reduce anxiety and feelings of depression and loneliness. And in a spiritual sense, it is healthy to take the focus off of yourself and be involved in the events of someone you love. As song artist Colton Dixon states, *"More of You, less of me. Make me who I'm meant to be. You're all I want, all I need, You're everything"* as he speaks of his relationship with God, his King.

Socializing also stimulates your mind and energy and helps cognitive function. It is a good opportunity to share thoughts, feelings, emotions, hobbies, concerns, ideas, time, and love. It is a human need to feel loved and accepted by others, so spending time nurturing your relationships is important. As discussed in previous chapters, be selective about your "circle of friends," and make sure you align yourself with like-minded people. This will eliminate unnecessary anxiety and tension in your life and promote only healthy and supportive relationships.

Sometimes the "best medicine" for a challenging circumstance in your own life is to take the focus off of yourself and instead direct your attention to how you can help someone else. Quite often, as you are consumed with a problem of your own, when you take your busy mind off of that problem and focus on caring for the needs of another person, you are blessed with compassion, creative thinking, solutions, and kindness given forth to the one you are helping and ultimately spilling over into your own situation. God commands us to love and help one another, and when we align ourselves to this higher calling, we will be blessed in return. Scripture actually tells us there will be blessings for those seeking to help and serve others.

Carry each other's burdens, and in this
way you will fulfill the law of Christ.
—Galatians 6:2 NIV

You are designed to interact with others; doing this face-to-face is best. Unfortunately, technology has become an increasingly convenient method of communication, taking over the true socialistic action of present human intimate contact. Socializing in person builds self-confidence and greater self-esteem and provides a deeper sense of comfort, contentment, and coping mechanisms. Participation in this type of communication is fading away behind the noise and distractions of electronic devices. Unfortunately, the release of serotonin and other "reward hormones" are causing droves of people to develop addictions to this form of technological stimulation.

Open your mind to the concept of spending more time with like-minded people. In both a business and personal sense, your life will be enriched in each scenario. You will learn different insights and ideas, enhance motivation, find peace and comfort in the company of another, and can share in the joy of lighthearted laughter.

It's all about being a part of something
in a community, socializing with people

*who share interests and coming together
to help improve the world we live in.*
                                        —Zach Braff

Social support tends to alleviate the effects of stress.
                                        —J. B. Cohen

*Encourage, lift and strengthen one another. For
the positive energy spread to one will be felt by
us all. For we are connected, one and all.*
                                        —Deborah Day

With the exponential progress of today's technology, it is imperative to be innovative and a valuable asset in the business world. This can be an exhausting endeavor to employ such creativity on demand. This chapter shared methods to increase your capacity to be innovative, including inspiring others, taking care of yourself in the form of quiet time, and taking time to socialize and nurture your relationships. It is important to take time to care for yourself and let your mind be relaxed and open to the flow of new ideas. Being inspirational displays and reinforces many qualities of a true leader. Not only is it effective for others, but you continue to grow in your own development as you empower others on their journey to success.

Prayer

LORD, thank You for letting me work with You to share Your joy with the world. Help me to be an inspiration to others as well as myself. Teach me to steward the talents and creativity You have entrusted to me and utilize them to bless others. May I use my creativity to glorify You and lift up Your name in all that I do. Help me to have eyes to see the needs around me and to respond to those needs with joy, hope, and inspiration. Help me also to realize the importance of my own health and the value of my own quiet time to rejuvenate my body, and mind. Thank You also for the loving relationships in my life and the ability to socialize with like-minded people. Thank You so much, Lord, for Your love and care over me. In Jesus's name. Amen.

Exercise

Close your eyes and focus on your breathing. Feel your heart and mind come together in sync. Focus on words such as love and light in your mind and heart. Repeat words of this kind, such as *Jesus, love, light,* and *angels.* "Fill my energy with love. Fill me with light." Imagine an aura of light surrounding you, growing brighter and brighter. Choose every thought carefully and only select high-energy, high-vibration light thoughts. Choose peace, joy, serenity, calmness, and self-control.

Feel the light energy expand around you. Let it flood your heart, mind, and entire body with positive high-frequency energy, and let it flow into your surroundings. If a negative thought comes to mind, let it flow through you, but do not let it attach to anything. Refocus on positive, loving things, and visualize the bright light and powerfully positive energy surrounding you and lifting you up.

Reflection

1. When confronted with an issue each day, think of two innovative options for resolving the problem and your rationale for these ideas.
2. Set aside fifteen to thirty minutes today away from distractions and allow your mind to rest. Choose to quiet your mind completely or just be alone with your thoughts. Practice doing this daily, in one form or another.
3. Find three ways today you can inspire someone else. Do you feel more energized, refreshed, and inspired as a result?

Wisdom from the Word

> *God is not unjust; He will not forget your work*
> *and the love you have shown Him as you have*
> *helped His people and continue to help them.*
> —Hebrews 6:10 NIV

> *And do not forget to do good and to share with*
> *others, for with such sacrifices God is pleased.*
> —Hebrews 13:16 NIV

> *Not looking to your own interests but each*
> *of you to the interests of the others.*
> —Philippians 2:4 NIV

CHAPTER 9

Passionately Energized

Passion

Passion is a strong emotion that energizes a person to pursue or not pursue something. It is a deep desire fueled by energy. The same passion can push you through difficult times or thrust you into a successful journey of intrigue and undiscovered dreams. A secret to living a dream is hidden in your passion and what you do with it. *"Among the traits and abilities that lead to success, passion stands alone."*[53] Unlike a skill or knowledge, it cannot be learned. It is something from within.

Passion is an overwhelming drive to reach your goals. It powers the hard work, determination, and creativity that make great accomplishments possible. Passion correlates with your desire and capacity to go above and beyond "normal" to achieve extraordinary outcomes. And without a doubt, passionate people contribute more than those without such a drive.

Passion can power you over difficult hurdles or setbacks, fueling you to generate a desire to learn, adjust, and try again. It generates the enthusiasm needed to plow through obstacles and overcome challenges. Passion also drives you to seek your deep desires and capitalize on your talents, gifts, and abilities. It is a thirst for the pursuit of something you crave, and it inspires loyalty, teamwork, hard work, and success.

Not only is passion of value for new pursuits, but it is also advantageous to use it to design solutions to old problems. Consider an instance, project, or process that has become stagnant. Let your passion out of the box and use it to find a way to create value, allowing motivation and interest to fuel your endeavor. Passion won't instantly create success, fortune, or fame. However, it allows you to persevere where others may give up, as the road to success is often quite long and bumpy. As you persevere, you will gain insights to avoid previous mistakes, and you will gain confidence as your creativity overflows to solve problems and improve processes.

Using your passion and learning as you proceed will also give you new and exciting roads to travel. It will reveal what you truly love to do. You may "fall forward" into a better fit for your life, using your interests to create new value, giving you that edge or advantage you need.

Passion is a key to your success. If you truly desire to be successful, this is a vital part of your blueprint. Are you passionate about your current career position? From a business perspective, what are you passionate about doing? What comes easily to you or makes you light up at the sheer thought of it? What is stopping you from the pursuit of this? How can you successfully use this passion? Fill out that application you've been putting off. Contact five successful people you know, and find out how they think. Make ten more cold calls today than usual. Follow up on fifteen more leads. Take steps to begin the business you only ever dreamt about. Do something about it *today*.

Read one new book per week. Begin harvesting your passion now. Say yes to offers before you even know how to work them out. Don't wait until tomorrow. When you have the passion, you will find a way. Do more, read more, listen more, give more, and think more than you've ever done before. It's time to get a little uncomfortable! You are completely energized and ready to push your threshold further than ever before. There is no better time than right now to get started.

> *A strong passion for any object will ensure success,*
> *for the desire of the end will point out the means.*
> —William Hazlitt

*My philosophy has always been, do what
you love and the money will follow.*
—Amy Weber

Initiative

Initiative is the ability to see something that needs to be done or addressed and taking the steps to do it without being instructed to do so. It is about going the extra mile…or two. This is an outstanding and desirable trait common in all successful people. *"Having initiative demonstrates a sense of self-drive, self-awareness, insight and personal motivation."*[54] It displays your true character and emulates the leader within you. This crucial skill will serve you well in both your professional and personal life.

Initiative can be learned, and a good start is by observing others who show initiative, observing the situation, and asking the right questions. Find out as much information as possible, and use your analytical skills to decide the best course of action. With initiative, you can identify opportunities and strengthen decision-making and analytical skills. You will serve as a role model for others.

Showing initiative is about being proactive rather than reactive. You learn how things work and also discover more efficient ways of doing things. By observing other successful people, you will become even more inspired to show initiative.

How to Take Initiative at Work:[55]

1. *Be proactive.* Anticipate what work needs to be done and do it before you are asked.
2. *Find opportunities for improvement.* Look for opportunities for improvement, such as weak points, the feedback you've received, or a pattern that is out of sync. Be constantly looking for something to present itself.
3. *Voice your ideas.* Expressing your opinion can help you establish your voice and build your rep-

utation as a person who looks for solutions. Offer suggestions and build your confidence as you share your ideas.

4. *Be decisive.* Be direct and choose the best way to proceed. Weigh the pros and cons and make the best decision you can under the circumstances.

5. *Improve systems, procedures, and policies.* Be aware of your environment and utilize forward-thinking, such as anticipating the need to update policies or procedures or identifying where improvements may be helpful or needed.

6. *Address and prevent problems.* Actively address issues as they occur, or anticipate them and find the root cause of the problems. Brainstorm independently or collaboratively to find the best solution to the problem. Can you identify a method of prevention?

7. *Be prepared for meetings.* This demonstrates that you've taken the initiative and put time and thought into the meeting's purpose.

8. *Anticipate questions and prepare answers.* Show initiative by always being prepared for any situation. Identify actionable ways to avoid issues in the future. Always stay two to three steps ahead.

9. *Set realistic standards.* Try to only take initiative on tasks that you have the time, energy, and resources to contribute to. You may participate in brainstorming other tasks, but if you know you are unable to participate fully, be responsible enough not to overextend yourself.

Success depends in a very large measure upon
individual initiative and exertion, and cannot
be achieved except by a dint of hard work.
—Anna Pavlova

*Your success is your responsibility. Take the
initiative, do the work, and persist to the end.*
—Lorii Myers

The power of writing it down

As you know, setting goals is a non-negotiable step for successful people. To take that one giant step further, rather than an annual January resolution to set or update your goals, make goal-setting a *daily* event! That's right, I said *daily*. Choose a time of day, either the beginning or the end of the day. Pick the one that you are most likely to commit yourself to. For the sake of choice, I'll focus on the first part of the day. Write it down. I start every morning by grounding myself in the Word. As you will see in the following chapter, the Bible is *full* of advice for *extreme* success professionally, personally, and spiritually.

Once grounded, I review my to-do list from the previous day and write out my goals (again) and the list of items I plan on accomplishing that day. This is a daily event to rewrite my goals, plus the "to-do" list that will lead to their accomplishment. The goals are longer-term events, and there is no better way to speed up the process of goal accomplishment than to rewrite them *every* day.

As was mentioned many times already, where attention goes, energy flows, and actions show. If you focus on your goals *every* day, both your conscious and subconscious minds will continually search and discover creative ways to make them come to fruition.

*But seek first the kingdom of God
and His righteousness, and all these
things will be added to you.*
—Matthew 6:33 ESV

Earlier, we also discussed the importance of declarations. Write down as many declarations that you find helpful that align with your goals. Read them aloud a few times every day, along with the goals.

What gets written gets done. Do not be afraid to write goals that appear out of reach or bigger than you believe possible. Whatever you think is reasonable, double it! Maybe even triple it! Wouldn't you rather slightly fail to reach a triple goal than slightly fail to reach a reasonable goal? When you strive for more with the right attitude and intentions, your thoughts continually work to help get you there. Watch enthusiastically as things become easier and start to fall into place, and goals are achieved well under the predetermined time-frame and at levels greater than expected.

By writing things down, you have recorded verbatim what was on your mind. It immediately has your attention in black and white and cannot be forgotten or misrepresented. This process clears your mind with a sense of relief as the pressure is lifted from retaining and remembering the information. Your thought process is now trans-formed into the mode of organizing and moving toward resolving the information.

Written down, it is now easier to prioritize and clarify your goals and intentions regarding this issue or topic. You are able to more clearly evaluate the next step in processing the information. Writing things down will allow you to maintain your resolve and remind yourself of your purpose regularly, so long as you keep it visible as a reminder. Daily progress is encouraged as you reread the contents of the list daily, along with your goals, and strive to clear off and address the listed items as soon as possible.

Clearly beneficial to writing things down is the ability to tap into a different part of your brain. Now that your brain isn't as stressed or overwhelmed focusing on remembering these things, you have the ability to creatively explore the content in more of an ana-lytical or problem-solving process. Do not underestimate the value of "good ole pen and paper." Having a visible reminder, clear thought processes, and emotional stability are invaluable assets in contribut-ing to the journey of your success.

*Decide what it is you want, write it down,
review it constantly, and each day do something
that moves you toward those goals.*
—Jack Canfield

*A goal that is not written is not a goal. It
only becomes real when you write it down.*
—Bryant McGill

*Top people have very clear goals. They
know who they are and they know what
they want. They write it down and they
make plans for its accomplishment.*
—Brian Tracy

Decisiveness

Indecision can be exhausting and frustrating. Decisiveness is an especially desirable skill in the business world. *"Few people put their trust in a person who overthinks and protracts the most basic of decisions—it makes us question their knowledge and experience. We're far more likely to put our trust in a person who knows where they are going and who can make clear, confident decisions, than to put our faith in somebody who is paralyzed by indecision."*[56]

Some benefits of being decisive include the following:

- *Reducing procrastination*
- *More productivity*
- *More organized*
- *More peace of mind*
- *Decreased anxiety*
- *Improved confidence*

Knowing how to be decisive is a trait of true leaders. It shows confidence, competence, and charisma when you commit to a decision. As Tony Robbins says, *"It is in your moments of decision that your destiny is shaped,"*—and we all want to shape our own destinies in extraordinary ways.

Many decisions you make daily are determined by your habits. Tony also says, *"Learning how to be decisive when it matters leads us down a path of confidence, fulfillment and joy—while being indecisive will cause us uncertainty, pain, and suffering."* And being decisive isn't even about being right. Even if you are wrong, you will come out a better person. Decisive people embody many strong and appealing qualities, such as being resilient, having lots of inner strength, being excellent problem solvers, and making great leaders.

Now the biggest question is, how do you become more decisive? Fortunately, being decisive is a skill that you can practice. Tony shares that there are a few steps that can be taken, starting with your mindset.[57]

1. *Overcome your fears.* If you are indecisive, you probably have some underlying fears. Decisions generally involve a change of some sort. Work toward being open to change rather than being fearful of it. Acknowledge and learn to accept that things are constantly changing, and take control of this fear and your life.

2. *Stop overanalyzing.* You generally learn more from a wrong decision than from a right one. It is okay to make mistakes. People are very forgiving, and more often than not, people are rooting for each other to do well. For example, think of when someone falls in a competition. The bystanders cheer when that person gets up and continues the race. Often, they cheer even more for that person than other competitors and see them through until the finish line. So do not be afraid of making a mistake. A poor decision often leads to a better one down the road. True leadership derives from the ability to make a decision, even when you are unsure whether or not you are right.

3. *Visualize the outcomes.* You can apply visualization concepts to decision-making, just like you do for goal-achiev-

ing strategies. Visualize positive, negative, and even neutral outcomes. This process will continue to condition your mind for quicker and easier decisions in the future.

4. *Make smaller decisions.* Practice is the key to your decision-making "muscles." If a big decision seems too overwhelming, break it down into smaller decisions. This will give you more decision-making practice and help condition you in the process.

5. *Don't chase perfection.* Perfection is another way that fear controls your choices. Sometimes "good enough" is the "perfect" answer. Perfection itself is an obstacle to decision-making. Think rather of some options that may get you closer to the goal. You do not have to have all the answers immediately. What's important is to have "an" answer and deliver it at the moment it is needed. You can always adjust, improve, or add to your decision later. If you need to, you can further visualize the consequences if your decision isn't completely accurate. I would venture to say everything ended up just fine. Consider the decisions as stepping stones rather than urgently needing to be right answers.

6. *Back your decisions with action.* Make it your decision to be decisive and move forward boldly with further actions to confirm or adjust the outcomes of this choice. Follow through until you see the results you desire. Be confident in yourself.

7. *Educate yourself.* The best leaders learn everything they can about a situation, job, circumstance, or opportunity and learn all of the skills necessary to be effective in every situation. Learn from books, blogs, other leaders, or mentors. Find an accountability partner to share in your decision-building quest. Successful people constantly look to improve their knowledge and skills and gather as much information as possible.

8. *Take massive action.* As Tony says, *"A real decision is measured by the fact that you've taken a new action. If there's no action, you haven't truly decided."*

Fear of failure is the biggest obstacle to becoming more decisive. Making a decision to improve your decisiveness is a life-changing action. It is a skill that can be mastered but must be practiced. If you take the time and put lots of effort into mastering this skill, you will never regret the benefits that result from it in both your professional and personal life.

> *Nothing is more difficult, and therefore*
> *more precious, than to be able to decide.*
> —Napoleon Bonaparte

> *A true leader has the confidence to stand*
> *alone, the courage to make tough decisions,*
> *and the compassion to listen to the needs of*
> *others. He does not set out to be a leader,*
> *but becomes one by the equality of his*
> *actions and the integrity of his intent.*
> —Douglas MacArthur

Massive action

A person can only become successful if they *take action—massive* action. You have assuredly previously heard about all of the qualities, characteristics, and obstacles outlined in the previous chapters. Reminders like this are imperative to help move and inspire you to action. You are armed with every weapon you need in your arsenal for success. Now you need to make a new blueprint for your journey, as your old one was less effective than you would have liked it to be. That's what this journey is all about—discovery.

You've discovered some helpful ideas from your past and found some that weren't a good fit for you. All of this is valuable information. Do not disregard any of it. It's all about trying something, implementing, observing, adjusting, learning what doesn't work, then modifying and discovering new ways that may be a better fit for your personality and goals. What works for someone else may not be the best approach for you or vice versa. The more information you have and the greater action you take, the higher the probability will be that you establish the appropriate building blocks to thrust you down the pathway to success—your success—designed specifically for you.

Personally, indecisiveness was my biggest obstacle. And what that boiled down to was not having a clear definition of what my goals were. I was diligent in preparing my annual January resolution goals. Almost diligent. I missed a few years in between. I would have to dig through my closet and find the black binder, which was divided into five sections—dreams, goals, values, motivational quotes, and daily to-do lists. It sounds fairly effective. However, the key ingredient was missing—*action!*

I will say that my results were equivalent to the amount of action I put into this exercise, which was minuscule. I could be embarrassed to admit this, yet as I discussed in this book, the past is the past, and the only time that really matters, where you can make a difference, is now and the future. I chose to learn from my past mistakes and grow *because* of these obstacles rather than live in regret. There is no justification for regret if you learn from your experiences and use them in a positive light to energize and motivate you to further *massive* action.

Be grateful for your past experiences. Praise God for all that you have experienced. Everything from your past has led you up to today, this very moment, with a new and powerful desire to succeed. This is not despite your past experiences but *because of* them. You are right where you are supposed to be at this moment. Get excited about the possibilities. Regarding my inactivity previously mentioned, once I clearly defined my goals and put them in writing as a twenty-page business plan, I knew exactly what I needed to do. I aligned my business plan with my values, morals, and ethics. I aligned it to who I am, where I am, and where I want to go. Now there is no more indecision. Along with practicing the methods to overcome indecision listed prior, I put it all into writing.

With every decision that needs to be made, I refer to my business plan, and the answer flows through my subconscious and conscious minds on autopilot. I have also defined my plan from a personal and spiritual level as well, allowing the same results. Since I have clearly defined values, goals, and ethics, my responses are second nature and already programmed in my mind, as discussed in previous chapters.

The worst decision you can make is to do nothing. Unless, of course, that is a deliberate choice that aligns with your values under a certain circumstance. Have you defined your goals? Do you rewrite them daily? Do you have a written business plan? How about a blueprint for your personal and spiritual life? Do you establish a daily written to-do list that aligns with your goals professionally, personally, and spiritually? When you commit to your mission of being successful, it will be difficult to accomplish unless all areas of your life are being addressed and are aligning with your values.

What actions can you take today to bring clarity to your plan for success? Do you know exactly what the definition of success is to you? If it's not written down, it will not happen. Or at least less likely. Put the odds in your favor and make it happen. Start to journal and write things down. Write as much down as you can. Take *massive* action! And take it *now!*

What was the turning point for you that allowed you to say you've had enough and want to see and make things change? Was it one event or a series of events? Was it based on something negative or something positive? If it was from something negative, transform that negative energy and utilize it under controlled circumstances in a powerful way. Let your vengeance be to become wildly successful. Naturally, you must do it for yourself and the right reasons. But if negative energy lurks, jump all over it, transforming it into a useful and productive form.

Energy is neither created nor destroyed; rather, it is transformed. If the event leading to the desire for change was already positive, sequester this favorable energy and raise it even further to high-frequency energy, and you will be unstoppable!

Do not wait any longer. The time for action is now. Start with your outlined written plans, read aloud your selected declarations daily, write your current actions, and rewrite your goals *daily*; continue to educate yourself from every source imaginable, read this book repeatedly, practice the exercises and reflections, and start saying yes to everything. Raise your energy to high-frequency, trust in your Holy Father that He wants you to succeed in everything you do, internalize and offer up the prayers daily, and start taking *massive* action!

> *You don't have to be great to start, but*
> *you do have to start to be great.*
> —Zig Ziglar

> *The path to success is to take*
> *massive determined action.*
> —Tony Robbins

> *Each of us must do massive right thinking,*
> *take massive right action and get massive*
> *right results, right here, right now.*
> —Mark Victor Hansen

In this chapter, energy is ramped up as we look at more active ways to pursue your goals, involving the mastery of passion, initiative, and even the power of massive, unstoppable action! Helpful skills relevant to your arsenal, making success possible, occur by becoming relentlessly decisive and putting thoughts, ideas, goals, problems, and potential solutions into writing. The time has come to take action. Recite your declarations, practice your exercises, and make your decision to keep persevering unconditionally toward your goals.

Prayer

> *Thank you, LORD, for equipping me with your*
> *strength; a strength I don't deserve and could never*

be capable of on my own. Thank you for carrying me when I am weak. Thank you for holding my hand when I'm too scared to take the next step. Thank you for lighting the way in the bleak darkness of my reality. Thank you for the instructions to be strong and take action. I know that these two go hand in hand. I know that I must not only be strong, but I must also take action.

Thank you for the strength that motivates me into action. I know that without action, I am simply stuck in a holding period. I know that without action, I am simply stuck. LORD, I pray to be like Ezra. I know that I am sinful. I pray for the audacity to confess boldly, repeat loudly, and lament intensely in front of others. I want to be strong and take action. I refuse to live in a holding period.

I pray that You equip me with Your strength that can carry me into action, and I pray that I can use a whole lot of exclamation points to describe how amazing You are. Thank you, LORD, for designing me to be exactly who I am. Thank you for Your strength that leads to action, especially in such uncertain times. Amen.[58]

Exercise

Close your eyes and focus on your breathing. Feel your heart and mind come together in sync. Focus on words such as love and light in your mind and heart. Repeat words of this kind, such as *Jesus, love, light,* and *angels.* "Fill my energy with love. Fill me with light." Imagine an aura of light surrounding you, growing brighter and brighter. Choose every thought carefully and only select high-energy, high-vibration light thoughts. Choose peace, joy, serenity, calmness, and self-control.

Feel the light energy expand around you. Let it flood your heart, mind, and entire body with positive high-frequency energy, and let it flow into your surroundings. If a negative thought comes to mind, let it flow through you, but do not let it attach to anything. Refocus on positive, loving things, and visualize the bright light and powerfully positive energy surrounding you and lifting you up.

Reflection

1. Name three things that came to mind as you read through this chapter that you are most passionate about. How can you turn any or all of them into something successful?
2. Name two things you have been putting off that it is now time to take initiative toward completing.
3. Name five steps of massive action you will take now as a result of this chapter. And I mean *now!*

Wisdom from the Word

> *Get up, for this matter is your responsibility,*
> *and we support you. Be strong and take action!*
> —Ezra 10:4 CSB

> *A slack hand causes poverty, but the*
> *hand of the diligent makes rich.*
> —Proverbs 10:4 ESV

> *I press on toward the goal to win the*
> *prize for which God has called me*
> *heavenward in Christ Jesus.*
> —Philippians 3:14 NIV

CHAPTER 10

Spiritually Empowered

The power of the Word

The Bible is full of business advice in all areas, including how to handle money. It is stated that *"every business owner should build their business on these essential principles straight from the Word of God."*[59] These principles include the following:

1. *Conduct your business with humility.* Humility allows you to listen to your clients, customers, or coworkers and hear their concerns, ideas, or suggestions. Having a large ego will only inhibit this valuable information.

   > *Pride goes before destruction, a*
   > *haughty spirit before a fall.*
   > —Proverbs 16:18 NIV

2. *Be diligent and avoid laziness.* Find work that you can be passionate about, even if this means departing your current position. No matter what it is, be diligent. Laziness is costly. Ensure you are well-rested, exercise regularly, and eat a healthy diet.

> *Lazy hands make for poverty, but*
> *diligent hands bring wealth.*
> —Proverbs 10:4 NIV

3. *Be fair and don't cheat in your business dealings.* From either a buyer's or seller's perspective, be on the same page with each transaction, giving full disclosure in every part of it, from description to the financial exchange.

> *Do not have two differing weights in*
> *your bag—one heavy, one light.*
> —Deuteronomy 25:13 NIV

4. *Gather little by little.* Gather money honestly, little by little. It may occur that there is a windfall of money, but most often, this is not the case. The Bible tells us that our focus should be on earning money little by little.

> *Dishonest money dwindles away, but whoever*
> *gathers money little by little makes it grow.*
> —Proverbs 13:11 NIV

5. *Don't be timid.* You can be humble and bold simultaneously. The Holy Spirit can give you the power to run your business and the self-discipline to manage your time.

> *For the Spirit God gave us does not make us timid,*
> *but gives us power, love and self-discipline.*
> —2 Timothy 1:7 NIV

> *So in everything, do to others what you*
> *would have them do to you, for this*
> *sums up the Law and the Prophets.*
> —Matthew 7:12 NIV

God is always and forever bigger than any problem you have ever or ever will encounter. Choose to be rich in spirit rather than poor in faith. If you desire to improve your business or life, remember to stay rooted in the Word of God. This is the one book that contains all of the best business secrets that business leaders need to know to build a successful business and life. As Ken Gosnell says, the Bible contains *"words for encouragement, consolation, improvement, and inspiration."* And it also contains the best principles for building a successful business. Some principles from Ken include the following:[60]

1. *Always take the second step.* Go a little further and do more than anticipated—and expected. Surprise others by paying attention to the little things that others don't. *"If someone forces you to go one mile, go with him two miles"* (Matthew 5:41 BSB). Too many businesses expect second-mile results without giving second-mile effort.

2. *The Golden Rule works if you work it.* Think of others first. Treat others like you would like to be treated. Practice thoughtfulness. *"Do to others as you would have them do to you"* (Luke 6:31 NIV). Companies that do not think of their customers will not be thought of by their customers.

3. *Focus on profit with a purpose.* Run your business with purpose and vision, knowing your priorities. Well-used profit can lead to both success and significance. Profit is great, but profit used for good is even greater.

> *What good is it for someone to gain the*
> *whole world, yet forfeit their soul?*
> —Mark 8:36 NIV

4. *Know your yesses and nos.* Be decisive and make decisions based on your values. Being wisely decisive is a key to influential leadership. Live up to your word. Build trusting relationships.

*And do not swear by your head, for you cannot
make even one hair white or black. All you
need to say is simply 'Yes' or 'No'; anything
beyond this comes from the evil one.*
—Matthew 5:36–37 NIV

5. *Move from ownership to stewardship.* "Well done" are two of the most powerful words in the English language.

    *Well done, good and faithful servant! You
    have been faithful with a few things; I will
    put you in charge of many things. Come
    and share your master's happiness!*
    —Matthew 25:23 NIV

6. *Trust the law of sowing and reaping.* Be generous with your seeds, plant daily, and sow bountifully. Constantly try new things. The harvest you reap today is from the seeds that you planted yesterday. The smallest mustard seed one day can produce the largest tree.

    *The point is this: whoever sows sparingly
    will also reap sparingly, and whoever sows
    bountifully will also reap bountifully.*
    —2 Corinthians 9:6 ESV

    *Remember this—a farmer who plants only a
    few seeds will get a small crop. But the one who
    plants generously will get a generous crop.*
    —2 Corinthians 9:6 NLT

    The point is to sow generously and consistently! Be patient, and do not give up. As Charles Stanley says, "*We reap what we sow, more than we sow, and later than we sow.*"

7. *Believe and ask for the impossible.* Dream bigger, pray bigger, ask for bigger, and expect bigger. Embrace bigger and stretch yourself and your business further.

> *Now to Him Who is able to do immeasurably*
> *more than all we ask or imagine, according to*
> *His power that is at work within us, to Him be*
> *glory in the church and in Christ Jesus throughout*
> *all generations, forever and ever! Amen.*
> —Ephesians 3:20–21 NIV

> *Everything is possible for one who believes.*
> —Mark 9:23 NIV

8. *Be forward-thinking.* Always do the right thing, and make decisions with tomorrow in mind. Your destiny unfolds based on your decisions today. Build on the right foundations and in a way to weather the storms. The time is always right to do what is always right. Act with integrity in every situation. If your business is built on a solid foundation, it will last generations.

> *Let your eyes look straight ahead; fix your*
> *gaze directly before you. Give careful thought*
> *to the paths for your feet and be steadfast*
> *in all your ways. Do not turn to the right*
> *or the left; keep your foot from evil.*
> —Proverbs 4:25–27 NIV

9. *Know the order of things and work the order.* Practice the art of first fruits in all aspects of your life. This should align with your values and priorities. Be clear and know the order of your priorities. Show clarity in all aspects of work and personal life.

*But seek first His kingdom and His righteousness,
and all these things will be given to you as well.*
—Matthew 6:33 NIV

10. *Improve your team to improve your organization.* First of all, select the correct people to be around you. Then learn from them. Grow with them. Help them discover their gifts, talents, and passions. Passionate people always perform better. And no great leader has ever led alone. It is only "lonely at the top" if you attempt to lead alone. Steward leaders believe in others and the power of others.

    *For we are God's handiwork, created in
    Christ Jesus to do good works, which God
    prepared in advance for us to do.*
    —Ephesians 2:10 NIV

    When the people you work with get better, so does your organization.

11. *Do things today that will impact tomorrow.* Invest in yourself, your people, your business, your associates, your family, your commitment, and your passion. Invest in all those that surround you. Good investments set the path and direction of a business, ensuring its growth and development. Where attention goes, energy flows, and actions show.

    *Where your treasure is, there
    your heart will be also.*
    —Matthew 6:21 NKJV

12. *Work to "well done."* Strive to make worthy and innovative work. Upgrade, improve, and keep current on all levels and in all areas. Show value and quality throughout your business and build this reputation consistently. Practice excellence at all times and in all situations, even during

challenges—especially during challenges. Excellent work is your eternal obligation.

> *Whatever you do, work at it with all your heart,*
> *as working for the LORD, not for human masters.*
> —Colossians 3:23 NIV

> *For this very reason, make every effort to add to*
> *your faith goodness; and to goodness, knowledge;*
> *and to knowledge, self-control; and to self-control,*
> *perseverance; and to perseverance, godliness;*
> *and to godliness, mutual affection; and to*
> *mutual affection, love. For if you possess these*
> *qualities in increasing measure, they will keep*
> *you from being ineffective and unproductive*
> *in your knowledge of our Lord Jesus Christ.*
> —2 Peter 1:5–8 NIV

Conviction

"*Conviction is a product of the relationship with God.*"[61] It is the fruit of a relationship. It is a quality that builds through your experiences, making something the center of your life. In a sense, it becomes your definition of what is right and what is wrong based on your vision, values, beliefs, and morals. The growth of your discernment depends on your day-to-day activities and the choices you make. Conviction-building actually began in your childhood and influences most of your actions today. "*Train up a child in the way he should go, and when he is old, he will not depart from it*" (Proverbs 22:6 JPS Tanakh 1917). *How* you think combined with *what* you think about helps produce the conditions and the activities you display externally.

"*The power of conviction is tremendous, and we all exercise it, to a varying degree.*" You have "*the power to decide between healing or illness, success or failure, great relationships or mediocre ones.*" It is also stated that *"the unequivocal belief in something helping engages our innate healing capacity."*[62] When you change the *way* in which you look at things, the things you look at change.

So, what are some of your convictions in your personal life? Can you name at least five? Can you expand that to ten? How do these convictions influence the decisions you make? How do they influence the relationships you have? Are there any changes you would like to make? Apply these same questions from a business perspective. Now apply them to a spiritual perspective. Are they all about the same?

Ground yourself

Grounding yourself means making yourself aware of the present moment. You aren't regretting the past or feeling anxious about the future. You are focused on what is happening to you right now. Being grounded allows you to calm your feelings and emotions and clear your busy mind, bringing you to the current moment physically, mentally, and spiritually. It also allows you to feel more in control of your life and circumstances.

There are many different techniques to ground yourself, and everyone responds differently to each technique. Grounding yourself is *"an opportunity to engage with your surroundings and pick apart your tangible qualities, and use to anchor your own state of being."*[63]

"As an exercise, it keeps your mind from wandering off outside the present and teaches you to focus on what is right in front of you." Some examples of *physical* grounding techniques are as follows:[63]

1. *Main technique: Five senses meditation.* This takes your mind off things you cannot control and brings you back to things you can. Focus on one thing and experience it vividly through the five senses. For example, take a few minutes to close your eyes (after you read this). What do you hear? Feel? Smell? Continue through each of the senses and try it while doing different things, such as showering, bathing, brushing your teeth, etc. By focusing on the pres-

ent moment, you train your mind to stay calm, relaxed, and aware.

2. *Eat really hot and really cold foods.* Follow this method with extreme temperatures and explore how your senses are affected.

3. *Try a "walk meditation."* As you walk, observe a mind-muscle connection with each step you take.

4. *Take deep breaths.* Bring awareness to your breathing and be intentional. When you allow stress into your day, your breathing becomes shallower. Changing to this type of intentional, slow, deep breathing allows you to become grounded once again. Notice a difference between breathing by expanding your chest versus expanding your belly (belly breathing) as uninhibited babies do. How does each way make you feel? Allow the oxygen to energize your muscles and clear your mind.

5. *Place your hands or feet in water.* Be mindful of any changes in temperature and how your skin feels.

6. *Hold a piece of ice.* Explore your senses. How long does it take to melt?

7. *Savor a scent.* What smell appeals the most to you? Bask in the qualities of this scent.

8. *Listen to your surroundings.* Enjoy the sounds of the birds. Are they chirping or singing? What other sounds do you hear?

A few suggestions for *mental* grounding techniques are listed:

- *Make yourself laugh.*
- *Visualize a task you enjoy.*
- *Keep a journal.*
- *Memorize or recite something.*
- *Picture someone you love.*
- *Pet your pet.*
- *Visualize a fun place you would like to visit.*
- *Visualize your problem disappearing or floating away.*

Examples of some *spiritual* techniques:

- *Listen to music.*
- *Focus on others.*
- *Touch something comforting.*
- *Pray.*
- *Meditate.*
- *Name or write down things you are grateful for.*
- *Listen to nature sounds.*
- *Listen to the sound of water.*

Being ungrounded is disassociating yourself from your mind and body. It is a type of defense mechanism. It happens to everyone at one point or another. The important thing is to recognize when you become ungrounded and find a technique that works for you, to bring you back to the present moment, and realign your thoughts and focus. This will become easier with practice.

> *Do your best to present yourself to God as one*
> *approved, a worker who has no need to be*
> *ashamed, rightly handling the word of truth.*
> —2 Timothy 2:15 ESV

> *When the Spirit of truth comes, he will guide you*
> *into all the truth, for he will not speak on his own*
> *authority, but whatever he hears he will speak, and*
> *he will declare to you the things that are to come.*
> —John 16:13 ESV

> *Get yourself grounded and you can navigate*
> *even the stormiest roads of peace.*
> —Steve Goodier

Spiritual integrity

Spiritual integrity is about being true to who you are. You are aware of what you want and align all choices and decisions with this value. There is an honest relationship with your feelings, and you embrace your human, vulnerable self. This is exemplified in all areas of your life and acts as a guide, simplifying your decision-making experience. While obstacles may arise to challenge a situation, using your spiritual integrity, you are able to transform the parts of you that characterize something as an obstacle. Aligning your actions with spiritual integrity is a freeing expression of your self-love as you abide by the "honor code" you designed for yourself.

"Spiritual integrity is the state of being undivided together with the quality of brutal self-honesty."[64] It is the combination of a state and a quality, which demands self-awareness and an uncompromising willingness to be authentic. This is not an easy undertaking! You must be humble, confident, reliable, open, and unceasingly honest. You must take responsibility for your blind spots and learn the skill of discernment along with humility and discretion so your mind may grow quiet enough to hear the direction of your values.

> *Wisdom is knowing the right path*
> *to take. Integrity is taking it.*
> —Anonymous

> *By consciously meditating upon spiritual*
> *truths and cultivating personal integrity, one*
> *need never fear negative circumstances.*
> —Aberjhani

The last yet most important tool in your shed for maximum success is in the power of the Word. Through the Word, you have every instruction necessary for a prosperous, productive, abundant, and successful life. You reviewed the tremendous power of conviction to keep you on the right path, methods to stay grounded, and the truth about exhibiting spiritual integrity through your character.

You are to embody each of these elements and let your success result from them all. The following chapter continues with the precious Word, utilizing the amazing power of prayer to transform, comfort, and energize your life.

Prayer

> *Thank you, LORD, for conviction, and thank you for loving me enough to pull me out of my sin. I pray, Father, for a heart that boldly walks in its convictions and leans into you. Help me, LORD, to see conviction as a gift, a gift of grace and mercy. Please continue to stir in my heart the places I've fallen complacent and lead me as I turn from them. Help me to live out the truth from Galatians 5:25, that if I say I live by the Spirit, let me stay in step with the Spirit. In Jesus' name, Amen.*[65]

Exercise

Close your eyes and focus on your breathing. Feel your heart and mind come together in sync. Focus on words such as love and light in your mind and heart. Repeat words of this kind, such as *Jesus, love, light,* and *angels.* "Fill my energy with love. Fill me with light." Imagine an aura of light surrounding you, growing brighter and brighter. Choose every thought carefully and only select high-energy, high-vibration light thoughts. Choose peace, joy, serenity, calmness, and self-control.

Feel the light energy expand around you. Let it flood your heart, mind, and entire body with positive high-frequency energy, and let it flow into your surroundings. If a negative thought comes to mind, let it flow through you, but do not let it attach to anything. Refocus on positive, loving things, and visualize the bright light and powerfully positive energy surrounding you and lifting you up.

Reflection

1. What is your "used for good" in the statement, "Profit is great, but profit used for good is even greater"? Practice being humble and bold at the same time.
2. Name three convictions regarding yourself or your business. If you do not currently have any, take some time to create them.
3. Name your top three methods for grounding yourself when necessary. Remind yourself of these methods and have them "at the ready" for when they are needed.

Wisdom from the Word

> *If we live by the Spirit, let us keep*
> *in step with the Spirit.*
> —Galatians 5:25 NIV

> *Trust in the LORD with all of your heart,*
> *and do not lean on your own understanding.*
> *In all your ways acknowledge Him, and*
> *He will make straight your path.*
> —Proverbs 3:5–6 ESV

> *My help comes from the LORD.*
> —Psalm 121:2 NIV

> *All Scripture is breathed out by God and*
> *profitable for teaching, for reproof, for*
> *correction, and for training in righteousness.*
> —2 Timothy 3:16 ESV

CHAPTER 11

Prayerfully Equipped

The power of prayer

"The power of prayer is, quite simply, the power of God, who hears and answers prayer. Prayer is the elevation of the mind and heart to God in adoration, in gratitude, and in a request for the spiritual and material things we need."[66] It creates a sense of union and relationship with God. The core of your character, who you become, and the circumstances of your life are all determined by what you talk to God about. Jesus tells us about the power of prayer in Matthew 18:18–20 (ESV):

> *Truly, I say to you, whatever you bind on earth shall be bound in heaven, and whatever you loose on earth shall be loosed in heaven. Again I say to you, if two of you agree on earth about anything they ask, it will be done for them by My Father in heaven. For where two or three are gathered in my name, there am I among them.*

If you understood the power available to you to take your authority in prayer, you would be praying in Jesus's name all the time! *"There would be no such thing as doubt, fear, or anxiety because we would be on our faces before God, storming the heavenly realms in battle with the darkness and evil forces in our world." "Prayer is an act of worship that glorifies God and reinforces our need for Him. Through living a life of prayer, we communicate with the very source of and purpose for our existence.*"[66]

It is the fiercest weapon you have against the enemy and all things of this fallen world. The power of prayer is actually the *power of God*, who hears and answers prayer. Just keep in mind that "No" or "Not yet" are also answers from God. He is not a genie who grants every wish exactly as you would like. Rather, He responds to what *He knows is best* for you, even if it's not the answer you desire. His ways are greater than our ways, and we often will not understand His reasons for our outcomes. He is beyond our understanding yet is always working for our ultimate good.

As we pray sincerely within our hearts, "*We experience the blessing of the presence of the Holy Spirit, and use it as light and strength for daily living—such are the fruits of true prayer.*"[66] Pray for growth, pray to give thanks, pray to seek forgiveness, and pray without ceasing. "*And pray in the Spirit on all occasions with all kinds of prayers and requests. With this in mind, be alert and always keep on praying for all the LORD's people*" (Ephesians 6:18 NIV).

Jesus made an unconditional promise to you when He said, "*Truly, truly I say to you, whatever you ask of the Father in my name, He will give it to you. Until now you have asked nothing in My name. Ask, and you will receive, that your joy may be full*" (John 16:23-24 ESV). You must be asking in alignment with His will for your life. He will not answer a request that may somehow harm you, and you may not understand this at the time of the answer. For example, if you ask for patience, He will allow circumstances to occur to grow your patience. The power of prayer rests in the power of God, not you saying the prayer. It's about being humble and filled with awe of the mighty Creator.

First John 5:14–15 (NIV) tells us, "*This is the confidence we have in approaching God: that if we ask anything according to His will, He hears us. And if we know that He hears us—whatever we ask—we know that we have what we asked of Him.*" You must come to the Father with confidence and full belief that He hears you and has the power to answer any request. In the gospel of Mark, he shares flaws in his own beliefs when he prays, *"I believe, help my unbelief."*

This is a request I pursue quite often to help ensure that I am placing full trust in His promises. My human nature sometimes places doubt in my own faith, and it is unimaginable even to begin to comprehend the immenseness and perfection of God, who is all truth.

Scripture says you are not to babble in your prayers, repeat incessantly, and say undue words if they aren't needed. God hears you the first time. And He already knows your heart. It is about spending time with Him in a relationship. *"And when you pray, do not keep on babbling like pagans, for they think they will be heard because of their many words. Do not be like them, for your Father knows what you need before you ask Him"* (Matthew 6:7–8 NIV). Prayers can be short and sweet. Right to the point.

Prayer is a conversation with God. I have been taught to begin with gratitude and praise to my heavenly Father for all He has allowed me to have and experience, especially for salvation through His Son, Jesus Christ. Then, when my energy and spirit are lifted from worship and appreciation, I present my requests to Him humbly and sincerely, submitting to His almighty power. I close the prayer with gratitude that He hears my prayer, and I believe He will answer according to His will, His timing, and what is best for my life. I sometimes include a request for my ability to be comforted and strengthened if the answer is not exactly as I had been hoping. A very important and most often overlooked part of praying is *listening.*

This is an active part of your conversation with God. It is a two-way communication. He speaks to you through other people, through Scripture, through occurrences in your life, and even through your thoughts and dreams. Bring yourself to an awareness of His still, quiet voice, and always be listening because He wants you to hear Him but waits for you to clear distractions and focus on Him before He speaks.

Pray daily for the success of your business, finances, growth and development, opportunities, motivation, wisdom, energy, ideas, relationships, your family, and every other part of your life. Pray that

God is all over your business and guides you to succeed profession-ally, personally, and spiritually. He wants you to be successful but also wants you to acknowledge that it all comes from and aligns with His power and grace and is ultimately for His glory.

> *But seek first the Kingdom of God*
> *and His righteousness, and all these*
> *things will be added to you.*
> —Matthew 6:33 ESV

While only the Holy Spirit can guide you to pray as you should, here are some suggestions on how to pray:[66]

1. *Pray with awareness.* Awareness gives you a genuine con-nection with God.
2. *Pray with humility.* Prayer with humility goes directly to the ear of God.
3. *Pray with love and grief.* Pray with delight and thanksgiving but also with authentic repentance and sincerity.
4. *Pray from the heart.* Even if you pray with the words of another, declare them as if they were your own.
5. *Pray with hope and total faith in God.* God knows your life and wants a relationship with you.

> *But when you pray, go into your room and shut the*
> *door and pray to your Father who is in secret. And*
> *your Father who sees in secret will reward you.*
> —Matthew 6:6 ESV

> *Therefore, confess your sins to one another*
> *and pray for one another, that you may be*
> *healed. The prayer of a righteous person*
> *has great power as it is working.*
> —James 5:16 ESV

Likewise the Spirit helps us in our weakness.
For we do not know what to pray for as we
ought, but the Spirit himself intercedes for
us with groanings too deep for words.
—Romans 8:26 ESV

Start with simple prayers. Sometimes the fewer words, the better. Talk to God in everyday language, as if speaking to a friend. Focus on your words and concentrate your attention on the conversation. Do not rush through them, but allow them to enter your heart. Often, your mind may begin to wander from the clutter of the day or evil forces that do not want you to succeed in a relationship with the Lord. Be gentle with yourself, refocus your attention, and try again.

Meditation

While prayer is speaking and listening to God, meditation is an act with the skill of removing the judgment component from thoughts and ideas. It involves relaxation, focus, and awareness. It is to the mind what physical exercise is to the body. *"It is a form of mental training or exercise whereby you exercise your brain to be relaxed."*[67] It is possible to meditate while focusing on God and His righteous nature or simply meditate to clear your mind, empty your thoughts, and raise your vibrations. Both are excellent options to reduce stress and bring peace and serenity into your life while allowing more focus and awareness. Meditation has been known to improve your performance and help keep you mentally and physically healthy. There are dozens of different ways to meditate. A few have already been discussed in previous chapters.

Here are a few steps on how to meditate:[67]

1. *Find a comfortable place to meditate.* Find a private, comfortable spot free from outside distractions or disturbances. Relax your muscles and remove all tensions and worries from your mind.

2. *Sit in a comfortable position and close your eyes.* Let the energy flow without obstruction. Close your eyes and take some deep breaths to calm your body. After a few cleansing breaths, you can breathe at a normal pace through your nose.

3. *Remove all thoughts from your mind.* Remove all thoughts from your mind and take more deep breaths to calm your mind. Loosen all of your body muscles and relax by the vibrations of any chosen chants if desired.

4. *Sit back and observe.* Observe your mind. You may allow it to think but do not engage actively. Be an observer of your mind.

5. *End the meditation.* End your meditation by slowly being present in the physical reality. Gradually get your mind and body attuned to the surroundings.

Be aware of your posture as you prepare to meditate and your chosen location so there are no interruptions and create an ideal atmosphere for your mind. Make sure your body and mind aren't too tired before you begin, and make sure you are wearing comfortable clothes. Have the right attitude and expectations as you meditate and link your values to this practice.

As you know, this book aims to elevate your mind to success. Meditation may be a method to clear your mind and prepare your mind and body for success. Seven Proven Ways Meditating Prepares You for Success:[68]

1. *Enhanced learning and memory.* Successful business leaders can quickly process and learn new information and recall that knowledge when needed. Meditation stimulates areas of the brain associated with memory, concentration, and learning. Mindfulness meditation helps increase gray matter volume, including bolstering areas of

the brain that assist in learning, memory, cognition, or emotional regulation. Meditation may actually change the brain's structure and increase mental activity and agility, making your brain more robust.

2. *Put a halt to pessimistic thought loops.* Obsessively dwelling on negative thoughts, such as past failures, frustrations, and regrets, can eat away at your confidence and cloud your mind. Meditation is a powerful aid in breaking these negative thought loops. You could even say a repeated mantra, such as "Let it go." Continue this phrase each time your mind wanders until the negative thought loop dissipates and frees your mind.

3. *Build mental capacity and improve accuracy.* Meditation is like a workout for your brain. Over time it can improve your overall brain health and build your mental capacity. Meditation can help sustain your focus, even during boring tasks. Meditating regularly not only increases your ability to concentrate but also boosts your attention to detail and level of accuracy.

4. *Tame negative emotions.* Meditation allows you to recognize and control negative emotions by helping you to process and accept what you are feeling, then assisting you in releasing those feelings. Mindfulness meditation, in particular, focuses on maintaining a moment-by-moment awareness of your thoughts, feelings, and bodily sensations with the surrounding environment. Accept the feelings that arise at the moment, then shed the emotions quickly for mental equilibrium.

5. *Create better relationships.* Through mindful meditation, you are better able to handle conflict when it arises, restabilize from mood swings, and accept your own emotions. You are more attuned

to yourself and your surroundings and have more emotional flexibility in how you respond.

6. *Remove stress and anxiety.* Meditation helps clear away the daily information overload that contributes to chronic feelings of stress. You are focused on one thing, such as breathing, which helps eliminate jumbled thoughts causing stress. It can provide you with a sense of peace, calm, and balance and help you gain a new perspective when facing a stressful situation.

7. *Tap into your creative side.* Meditation can help nurture the idea-making part of your brain. Let your mind jump from one thought to another without judgment or exerting control from within. This type of meditation will encourage creative thinking.

Focus your mind on the present, and visualize the outcomes you want, whether it's business success, personal growth, or other favorable goals. Meditation can help you focus, increase productivity, and influence your reactions. Master your emotions and frame your experiences in a positive light.

Prayer

> *Father God, I ask for your blessing on my life and the lives of my family. I pray that You would remove the sting of sickness and disease from those attached to me. I pray that You would increase my influence amongst Your people, LORD, that I may be able to glorify You more. I pray for abundance and prosperity in my home, in my church, in my career, and in my family. I know You are able to do abundantly, above which I ask or think and I thank You in advance. In Jesus' name, Amen.[69]*

Exercise

Close your eyes and focus on your breathing. Feel your heart and mind come together in sync. Focus on words such as love and light in your mind and heart. Repeat words of this kind, such as *Jesus, love, light,* and *angels.* "Fill my energy with love. Fill me with light." Imagine an aura of light surrounding you, growing brighter and brighter. Choose every thought carefully and only select high-energy, high-vibration light thoughts. Choose peace, joy, serenity, calmness, and self-control.

Feel the light energy expand around you. Let it flood your heart, mind, and entire body with positive high-frequency energy, and let it flow into your surroundings. If a negative thought comes to mind, let it flow through you, but do not let it attach to anything. Refocus on positive, loving things, and visualize the bright light and powerfully positive energy surrounding you and lifting you up.

Reflection

1. Talk to God conversationally five times today as if speaking to an intimate friend. Did this come naturally? If not, do not give up. But rather keep speaking with Him daily and observe how fluent it becomes.
2. Create or copy a prayer about your success that aligns with your values, and always keep it with you. Read and pray this prayer every morning before your day begins and at the end of each day.
3. Pray daily that your goals and agenda align with God's will for your life. Pray for discernment in all of your decisions.
4. Perform the meditation exercise presented at the end of each chapter daily, and allow it to clear your mind and free your thoughts. Use the previous suggestions to help prepare for an optimal meditation experience.

The Serenity Prayer is a wonderful prayer for all aspects of your life, including your business: "*LORD, grant me the serenity to accept the things I cannot change, the courage to change the things I can, and the wisdom to know the difference."*

Wisdom from the Word

> *Do not be anxious about anything, but in*
> *every situation, by prayer and petition, with*
> *thanksgiving, present your requests to God.*
> *And the peace of God, which transcends*
> *all understanding, will guard your hearts*
> *and your minds in Christ Jesus.*
> —Philippians 4:6–7 NIV

> *Rejoice always, pray continually, give*
> *thanks in all circumstances; for this is*
> *God's Will for you in Christ Jesus.*
> —1 Thessalonians 5:16–18 NIV

> *Therefore, I tell you, whatever you ask*
> *for in prayer, believe that you have*
> *received it, and it will be yours.*
> —Mark 11:24 NIV

CHAPTER 12

Undoubtedly Prepared

As we look back at your elevation journey, Chapter 1 began by defining the problem—your thoughts and your mind had been programmed by someone other than you. The state of your current mind was the basis of all of your decisions, including the level of success you had obtained up to that point. Once an awareness of the current state was established, it was necessary to define your belief system and core values and identify a direction in which to align decisions to your goals. These are the building blocks needed for a business or even life plan, especially for identifying who you really are and what is important to you. You were then encouraged to establish a specific written business plan for your career or business as a blueprint and direction from which to proceed.

This book's core and unique nature is in the awareness, instruction, and guidance on elevating your mind to success. In Chapter 2, you were presented with all things energy! You learned that your mind consists of energy, and it is in constant motion, neither being created nor destroyed but rather transferred and transformed. Energy is either positive or negative, and you have the ability to influence this condition and its frequency. You also read about vibrations and learned twelve ways to raise them, in addition to ways to change your frequency so you can attain your desired level of vibrational energy at any given time. You discovered that tranquility and calmness may also transpire as you read about the many benefits of achieving inner peace. You were then introduced to a particular meditation you were asked to perform from that chapter on to build and develop your muscle memory for harmonizing and balancing your mind, allowing it to relax upon your command or instruction.

With a higher level of consciousness comes a higher level of understanding. Chapter 3 continued with the elevated state of mind by sharing information regarding six levels of observation, how "life happens" with each of them, and how to identify them. This allowed you to see where your current level of awareness resided, giving you complete control over how you wanted to handle your current level. Contemplation can shift you into a state of higher consciousness. You were to consider how you felt about where you were and make decisions about where you wanted it to be. Praise and gratitude were then introduced as they both have a positive impact physically and psychologically and also have a way of elevating the energy in your mind. They are powerful methods of enlightening the spirit and promoting well-being.

The chapter closed with a final section regarding net worth and key reasons you need to be aware of it as a snapshot of your financial stability and overall picture of your financial health as we began to tie in the development of your character with the growth of your wealth in your transformation to success.

Learning is a lifelong process and is a key to success and opportunities in your life. In Chapter 4, you began to build on your foundation with the relevance and importance of essential factors in the navigational plan of your journey to prosperity, including education, money, and time management. These are invaluable tools necessary for building stable and consistent success in all aspects of your life and for your lifetime. Building a budget makes it possible to create an investment strategy and become aware of the heartbeat of your business or home expenses. Successful time management leads to greater personal happiness, increased accomplishments, and an abundant future. Ten strategies for better time management were provided in this chapter.

You again were encouraged to elevate your mind with the topic of spiritual wealth as being rich spiritually as the wealthiest type of rich possible. Passive income is vital for building net worth, even more so than an active income. Twelve benefits of passive income were outlined and described, with tips and suggestions on various possible venues for investment. The chapter concluded with inspiration to begin to think *big!* You were encouraged to think outside the box of extended possibilities and opportunities. Look at continual learning and growth in professional, personal, and spiritual aspects of your life. Do not limit yourself but rather remove self-limiting and negative thoughts and think *big!*

Obstacles will always be a part of your business environment. Every challenging situation is an opportunity to brainstorm for creative solutions. Chapter 5 introduced an array of obstacles you will encounter, such as physical and mental clutter, lack of focus, complacency, and bad attitudes. Clutter may lead to unwarranted impulses or feelings of loss of control. It is important to sort through the clutter and remove it from your mind and your physical workspace. Concentration exercises can help boost your ability to focus, and eliminating distractions or establishing a serene environment can provide a more suitable atmosphere for concentrating. Move forward in your learning and growing, and do not allow complacency to engage. A bad attitude must be addressed immediately and reframed with a positive and favorable outlook. Bitterness is a harmful emotion that needs forgiveness, and regret should be prevented from the get-go. Fear only holds the power you give it as it is a *f*alse *e*vent *a*ppearing *r*eal and has not actually happened. You have the power to control your thoughts over fear.

Let go of the unattainable goal of perfectionism and enjoy the accomplishments of your journey. You identified different types of toxic people and learned how to deflate their impact and dissolve their effect on your thoughts and mind and potentially even the need to eliminate them from your life! By utilizing the suggestions and practicing the exercises, you have become more efficient in overcoming each of these obstacles. You are equipped to dissolve their impact on your elevated journey to success.

The first step to reprogramming your mind is to know what you are reprogramming. The problem must first be exposed, and this occurs through honest awareness. In Chapter 6, you became honestly aware of your thoughts as part of this crucial process and flexibly open to a new perspective, including the benefits of taking a fresh approach. Knowing your personality is key to uncovering your true self. You identified your individual type of personality, specifically focusing on your strengths and weaknesses and how to utilize each to your successful advantage.

As meditation is important to reprogramming your mind, a small informative section was included, along with the regular meditation exercise at the end of this and all chapters. Many more traits are included to enhance the reprogramming and elevation of your mind, including responsibility, accountability, and being intentional. These are powerful and necessary traits found in every successful leader.

An informative explanation and application of neuroplasticity followed to help connect the dots on improving learning and memory, then suggestions on how to break bad, unwanted habits. The chapter continued with a comparison of affirmations versus declarations with an explanation of their differences and the benefits of setting appropriate boundaries, especially at work. The chapter concluded with encouragement to think even *bigger* yet! There is no room for regret on your elevation journey, and a vision is part of the optimal approach, especially a *big* vision, using your values as the platform for this important factor.

Listening allows you to see into the hearts and minds of other people. Chapter 7 shared the extreme importance and value of listening and open and honest communication. This is a trait that not everyone understands, yet it shines as an asset in every successful person. Fortunately, it is a skill that can be refined and cultivated as part of your own footprint. There is power in the ability to think freely and independently, yet having the flexibility of mastering the skill of compromise, knowing interactions are always most successful when each party feels satisfied with an agreed-upon outcome.

In this chapter, you were also impassioned to elevate your mind even further with the power of fully receiving a compliment, its intended encouragement, and the elevated effects of contentment and gratitude. Self-worth and confidence should be practiced and built up as suggested, just as your trustworthiness should be earned through your consistent actions.

Being innovative takes creativity and forward-thinking. In Chapter 8, it was time to be refreshed after your hard work and devotion throughout the first seven chapters. Elevate your mind with your innovation and curiosity, employing new perspectives and an openness to change. And remain elevated as you strive to inspire others and refresh your own soul with inspiration, quiet time, and social time of your own. It is important to accept this time of refreshment and the high-frequency energy that comes with it to rejuvenate your body, mind, and spirit as your mind is being reprogrammed with the help of this relaxed state of being.

Now while in a state of peaceful yet energetic abundance, Chapter 9 poured in the passion and energized you to take initiative, commit everything to writing, and take *massive* action! You know how to overcome hurdles and obstacles; you've already identified the problem and taken steps to reprogram your mind. You learned how to refresh your mind, body, and soul; now it's all about the action! There are no excuses given by successful people. There is no regret. There is no fear. If such a feeling begins to develop, instantly convert it into positive energy to fuel your flames of passion and desire to fulfill your goals.

You know how to be decisive and the value of this powerful trait. Don't wait. Make decisions, even if they are wrong. Take responsibility for your actions and correct them. In time, you will be so well-versed and practiced in all these skills that automatic right answers will be the rule, not the exception. Remember, the worst decision you can make is to do nothing at all.

The Bible itself is a strategy for success as it is full of business advice. Chapter 10 continued elevating your mind with the power of the Word. The Bible includes every detail needed to live and breathe a successful lifestyle from every perspective, including professionally, personally, and spiritually. Specific principles were defined regarding how to handle money and how to build a successful business. The chapter appropriately concludes by discussing conviction and techniques to ground yourself in the present moment, elevating your mind with a sense of calmness in your emotions and feelings. And, finally, your mind was elevated with spiritual integrity, aligning all choices and decisions with this value.

Prayer is the elevation of the mind and heart to God. You have the ability to take your authority in prayer at any and all times in your conversations through your relationship with God. The last informative chapter, Chapter 11, discussed prayer and meditation, some differences between them, and how they are each beneficial for success, including examples of how to perform each. While meditation had already been discussed throughout the book, new information was added to this chapter, including many beneficial ways meditation may be used in preparation for success.

Each chapter concluded with a meditation exercise to be performed upon its completion and also daily, along with a concluding prayer and reflection activities to complete for skill development and wisdom from the mighty Word.

You are undoubtedly prepared for an abundance of success and prosperity. If you followed the format and contents of this book, you have built upon the carefully designed structure and succeeded in elevating your mind, body, and spirit to a whole new level of success. It is *now* time to become fixated on success. Be committed, determined, and passionate about a positive outcome and victory. It's time to go "all in." You have all the skills, abilities, knowledge, and mindset needed to be successful. You cannot fail unless you quit. It takes consistency and persistence to reach goals.

As a reminder, this book is not meant to imply self-reliance in any way or any illicit "prosperity." All things are through Jesus Christ. Through Him alone and in His name, you are capable of achieving wonderful and abundant things. Put forth the appropriate effort necessary and discover and enjoy the amazing journey of an elevated mind.

There is no limit to the number of chances you can take, the energy you can commit, or the actions you can pursue. Lead the pack rather than follow the crowd. Be persistent in moving forward. Don't ever stop adding wood to your fire. Don't let obscurity be a problem. Be bold, intentional, make yourself known, and increase your footprint wherever possible. Use any fear that creeps in to fuel your fire and passion to succeed. Choose abundance in all areas of your life rather than balance, and prioritize it. Make it your duty and responsibility. Use your gifts, talents, and energy. Act now and cause people to think about you. Make your presence known, and make it known everywhere.

Commit to the successful achievement of your goals, and make all of your actions geared toward the pursuit of them. Choose wisely how you invest one of your most precious assets—your time. Have the attitude that a solution exists, no matter what. There are no obstacles you cannot overcome. You will grow and expand with each obstacle you successfully undertake. Be willing to take risks. In order to advance, you have to face danger and take high levels of risk. Taking this kind of action is something that can be practiced until it is a habit. You will get better and better at allowing massive action to become second nature.

Thank you for taking this journey of mind elevation. Reread or relisten to this book monthly for the first year to establish the skills as habits. Then continue to read or listen again at least once or twice a year. Share a copy of this book with others, and help them understand and relate to your new level of elevation and encourage them to grow. Do not stop growing, learning, and trying new things. Keep expanding and elevating your mind to success, prosperity, and abundance, and never, ever give up.

REFERENCES

1. Bakken, Earl E. 2016. "What Are Thoughts and Emotions?" takingcharge.csh. umn.edu https://www.takingcharge.csh.umn.edu/what-are-thoughts-emotions.

2. Teasley, Deborah. November 22, 2021. "Belief Systems: Definitions and Types." study.com. https://study.com/academy/lesson/belief-systems-definition-types-quiz.html.

3. DeHaas, Tao. September 1, 2011. "What Is a Belief?" aboutmybrain.com. https://www.aboutmybrain.com/blog/what-is-a-belief.

4. "The Importance of Defining your Core Values." September 15, 2021. souldistillery.com. https://www.souldistillery.com/blog-1/the-importance-of-defining-your-values.

5. Imafidon, Casey. 2022. "7 Habits You Should Learn from Successful People." lifehack.org. https://www.lifehack.org/301984/7-habits-you-should-learn-from-successful-people.

6. "Prayer for Achieving Goals." Prayerist.com. https://www.prayerist.com/prayer/achievinggoals.

7. "Prayer for Success." 2022. holylandprayer.com. https://www.holylandprayer.com/prayer_for/prayer-for-success/.

8. Poff, Sara Jo. December 22, 2017. "Frequencies and Energy—What Christians Need to Know." healthyfamiliesforgod.com. https://www.healthyfamiliesforgod.com/blog/2017/10/28/frequencies-and-energy-how-believeing-they-are-new-age-will-limit-your-christian-life.

9. "What Are the Benefits of Inner Peace?" October 19, 2021. Pearlmindz.com. https://pearlmindz.com/benefits-of-inner-peace/.

10. Kalev, Melani. January 16, 2018. "Understanding Positive and Negative Energy in People." blog.mindvalley.com. https://blog.mindvalley.com/positive-and-negative-energy/.

11. Maree, Gayle. 2022. "How to Protect Yourself with High-Frequency Energy." 6dimensionsofhealing.com https://6dimensionsofhealing.com/protect-yourself-with-high-frequency-energy/.

12. Beckler, Melanie. 2022. "Heart Coherence—Quickly Realign with Divine Love." ask-angels.com. https://www.ask-angels.com/spiritual-guidance/heart-coherence/#:~:text=Heart%20coherence%20is%20when%20your%20brain%20waves%20and,synchronized%20and%20moving%20together%20in%20an%20organized%20manner.

13. "Prayer for Energy." prayerist.com. https://prayerist.com/prayer/energy#:~:text=pray.

14. O'Malley, Mary. 2019. "The Six Levels of Higher Consciousness" consciouslifestylemag.com. https://www.consciouslifestylemag.com/the-six-levels-of-higher-consciousness-how-to-make-the-shift/.

15. Wommack, Andrew. 2022. "Effects of Praise." awmi.net. https://www.awmi.net/reading/teaching-articles/effects_praise/.

16. Cherry, Kendra. October 29, 2021. "What is Gratitude?" verywellmind.com. https://www.verywellmind.com/what-is-gratitude-5206817.

17. Common Sense Media. June 2, 2020. "What is Gratitude?" commonsensemedia.org. https://www.commonsensemedia.org/articles/what-is-gratitude.

18. Linda @ The Cents of Money. April 22, 2021. "10 Reasons Why You Should Know Your Net Worth." thecentsofmoney.com. https://thecentsofmoney.com/ten-reasons-why-you-should-know-your-net-worth/.

19. "Prayers of Gratitude: 17 Inspirational Powerful." 2022. thepraywarrior.com. https://thepraywarrior.com/prayers-of-gratitude-17-inspirational-powerful/.

20. "A Prayer of Praise and Gratitude—Your Daily Prayer." February 21, 2022. crosswalk.com. https://www.crosswalk.com/devotionals/your-daily-prayer/a-prayer-of-praise-and-gratitude.html.

21. The Spiritual Life LLC. 2022. "Prayers For Prosperity." slife.org. https://slife.org/prayers-for-wealth-and-prosperity/.

22. "10 Benefits Showing Why Education Is Important to Society." 2022. Habitat for Humanity. habitatbroward.org. https://habitatbroward.org/blog/benefits-of-education/.

23. Editorial Team. February 22, 2021. "What Is a Budget?" indeed.com. https://www.indeed.com/career-advice/career-development/what%27s-a-budget.

24. Chery, Fritz. July 25, 2022. "Time Management." biblereasons.com. https://biblereasons.com/time-management/.

25. "Time Management: 10 Strategies for Better Time Management." 2022. The University of GA. extension.uga.edu. https://extension.uga.edu/publications/detail.html?number=C1042.

26. "12 Benefits of Passive Income." January 14, 2021. beginnerspassiveincome.com. https://beginnerspassiveincome.com/benefits-passive-income/.

27. Connell, Laura. 2022. "Toxic People in the Workplace: How to Protect Yourself." laurakconnell.com. https://laurakconnell.com/toxic-people-in-the-workplace/.

28. Van Edwards, Vanessa. "7 Types of Toxic People." scienceofpeople.com. https://www.scienceofpeople.com/toxic-people/.

29. Brito, Janet PhD. November 20, 2019. "Do's and Don'ts for Dealing with Toxic Behavior." healthline.com. https://www.healthline.com/health/how-to-deal-with-toxic-people.

30. "Powerful Prayers for Being Confident." 2022. holylandprayer.com. https://www.holylandprayer.com/prayer_for/prayers-for-confidence/.

31. Editor in Chief. February 8, 2019. "7 Strong Spiritual Warfare Prayers for the Mind." connectusfund.org. https://connectusfund.org/7-strong-spiritual-warfare-prayers-for-the-mind.

32. Gould, Ed. 2022. "Changing Perspective and Gaining Happiness." happiness.com. https://www.happiness.com/magazine/inspiration-spirituality/perspective/

33. "9 Benefits of Receiving Fresh Perspectives in Business." myva360.com. https://myva360.com/blog/receiving-fresh-perspective-in-business.

34. 16 Personalities. 2022. 16personalities.com. https://www.16personalities.com.

35. Watson, Bron. 2022. "The Secret of Taking Responsibility Will Make You Successful." bronwatson.com. https://bronwatson.com/the-secret-of-taking-responsibility-will-make-you-successful/.

36. Gupta, Shreya. June 14, 2022. "Taking Responsibility for Your Actions: A Humble Beginner's Guide to Personal Growth and Leadership." xmonks.com. https://xmonks.com/taking-responsibility-for-your-actions/.

37. Devries, Lora. 2022. "7 Benefits of Intentional Living and The Importance of Being Intentional." loradevries.com. https://eee.loradevries.com/blog/Benefits-of-Living-Intentionally.

38. "Neuroplasticity." 2022. Psychology Today. psychologytoday.com. https://www.psychologytoday.com/us/basics/neuroplasticity.

39. Pandey, Erica. September 19, 2022. "How to Break a Bad Habit." axios.com. https://axios.com/2022/09/20/how-to-break-a-bad-habit.

40. Gevanter, Laura. July 26, 2011. "Affirmations Vs. Declarations." ezinearticles.com. https://www.ezinarticles.com/?Affirmations-Vs-Declarations.

41. Molitor, Michele. October 2022. "7 Unexpected Benefits of Setting Boundaries At Work." msn.com. https://www.msn.com/en-us/health/wellness/7-unexpected-benefits-of-setting-boundaries-at-work-exactly-how-to-do-it/ar-AA1213vV.

42. Potter, Ron. July 27, 2015. "6 Steps to Establish a Vision." teamleadershipculture.com. https://www.teamleadershipculture.com/blog/6-steps-to-establish-a-vision/.

43. "Listening—A Crucial Skill for Success." 2022. skillsyouneed.com. https://www.skillsyouneed.com/rhubarb/listening-for-success.html.

44. Alton, Larry. 2022. "7 Secrets for Better Compromise in the Workplace." inc.com. https://www.inc.com/larry-alton/7-secrets-for-better-compromise-in-workplace.html.

45. Ackerman, Courtney E. MA. November 6, 2018. "What Is Self-Worth and How Do We Build It?" positivepsychology.com. https://www.positivepsychology.com/self-woth/.

46. Bridges, Frances. July 21, 2017. "10 Ways to Build Confidence." www.forbes.com. https://www.forbes.com/sites/francesbridges/2017/07/10-ways-to-build-confidence/?sh=17a4bec23c59.

47. Erica. December 21, 2015. "The Importance of Being Trustworthy." twthonline.org. https://twthonline.org/the-importance-of-being-trustworthy/.

48. Kent, Keri Wyatt. 2022. "The Spiritual Practice of Trust." christianitytoday. com. https://www.christianitytoday.com/pastors/2011/may-online-only/ spiritualpracticetrust.html.

49. Stenta, Pastor Katy. March 28, 2022. "Fiercely Listening, a Prayer." katyandtheword.com. https://katyandtheword.com/2022/03/28/fiercely-listening-a-prayer/#:~:text=Fiercely%20listening%2C%20a%20prayer%20God%20sometimes%20I%20think,pray%20about%20all%20those%20without%20ears%20to%20hear.

50. Wooll, Maggie. March 8, 2022. "Inspire Others and Support Their Growth. 10 Ways to Make It Happen." betterup.com. https://wwwbetterup.com/blog/ how-to-inspire-others.

51. Latumahina, Donald. September 9, 2011. "7 Ways to Inspire Yourself." lifeoptimizer. org. https://www.lifeoptimizer.org/2011/09/09/ways-to-inspire-yourself/.

52. Lenahan, Kieran. January 21, 2021. "The Value of Quiet Time in the Age of Noise." lenahancoaching.com. https://www.lenahancoaching.com/shorticles/ value-of-quiet.

53. "Why Passion Is the Key to Success." May 11, 2017. tempstarstaffing.com. https://www.tempstarstaffing.com/2017/05/11/passion-key-success/.

54. Muguku, Duncan. 2022. "17 Tips on How to Take Initiative at Work." thriveyard. com. https://www.thriveyard.com/17-tips-on-how-to-take-initiative-at-work/.

55. Editorial Team. December 12, 2019. "9 Ways to Take Initiative at Work." indeed.com. https://www.indeed.com/career-advice/career-development/ ways-to-take-initiative-at-work.

56. The Wholegrain Team. May 22, 2015. "The Benefits of Being Decisive." wholegraindigital.com. https://www.wholegraindigital.com/blog/the-benefits-of-being-decisive/.

57. Team Tony. 2022. "How to be More Decisive." tonyrobbins.com. https:// www.tonyrobbins.com/stories/unleash-the-power/be-decisive/.

58. "A Prayer for Strength and Action: Your Daily Prayer." July 16, 2022. crosswalk. com. https://www.crosswalk.com/devotionals/your-daily-prayer/your-daily-prayer-july-16.html#:~:text=Whatever%20action%20may%20look%20like%20in%20your%20life%2C,could%20never%20be%20capable%20of%20on%20my%20own.

59. Lotich, Bob. 2022. "5 Essential Business Principles from the Bible." www1. cbn.com. https://www1.cbn/finance/5-essential-business-principles-bible.

60. Gosnell, Ken. January 13, 2018. "The 12 Biblical Principles on Which to Build a Business." linkedIn.com. https://www.linkedIn.com/ pulse/12-biblical-principles-which-build-business-ken-gosnell/.

61. Ritenbaugh, John W. 2022. "What the Bible Says About Conviction." Bibletools.org. https://www.bibletools.org/index.cfm//fuseaction/Topical. show/RTD/cgg/ID/838/Conviction.htm.

62. Geist, Katrin. September 7, 2014. "The Power of Convictions and How They Shape Our Lives." wakeup-world.com. https://www.wakeup-world.com/2014/09/07/the-power-of-convictions-and-how-they-shape-our-lives/.

63. Brown, Lachlan. March 3, 2022. "How to Ground Yourself: 35 Grounding Techniques to Calm Yourself Down." hackspirit.com. https://hackspirit.com/how-to-ground-yourself/

64. O'Keefe, Jac. March 4, 2020. "What Is Spiritual Integrity?" newharbinger.com. https://www.newharbinger.com/blog/spirituality/what-is-spiritual-integrity/.

65. "A Prayer for Walking in Your Convictions—Your Daily Prayer." January 13, 2022. crosswalk.com. https://www.crosswalk.com/devotionals/your-daily-prayer/a-prayer-for-walking-in-your-convictions.html.

66. Riggleman, Heather. April 21, 2020. "What Is the Power of Prayer?" christianity.com. https://www.christianity.com/wiki/prayer/what-is-the-power-of-prayer.html.

67. "Prayer and Meditation—Explained for All." 2022. adventistguide.com. https://adventistguide.com/prayer-and-meditation/.

68. Patel, Deep. July 25, 2018. "7 Proven Ways Meditating Prepares You for Success." entrepreneur.com. https://www.entrepreneur.com/living/7-proven-ways-meditating-prepares-you-for-success/316801.

69. "5 Powerful Prayers for Success in Business, School, Home and Life." 2022. undoubtedgrace.com. https://www.undoubtedgrace.com/prayers-for-success/.

ABOUT THE AUTHOR

Jill Fandrich, PharmD, received her doctorate in pharmacy from Shenandoah University in Winchester, Virginia, and her degrees in chemistry and pharmacy from Westminster College and the University of Pittsburgh, respectively. During this time, she was a noted and accomplished public speaker, presenter, educator, diabetes care specialist, writer, artist, performer, director of pharmacy, and media personality with a passion for helping people feel and live their best.

As an entrepreneur, Jill simultaneously became integrated into other endeavors of improving her community with house restoration and built corporations in the real estate and financial sectors, participating with other local entrepreneurs and businesses in joint cooperation of beautification.

Jill has most recently focused on her passion for writing to guide and encourage people and empower them to develop and discover their own unique and full potential. She is a writer, book reviewer, and author of *COVID-19 Prevention, Parents: COVID-19 Prevention for Kids,* and *A Book in Time Blog,* found at www.ABookinTime. net, where she educates, inspires, motivates, and energizes people to utilize their unique skills and abilities to bring about the leader and success potential already located from within.

When not writing, Jill can be found spending time with family and friends; traveling; golfing; currency trading; reading; running; playing tennis; fixing, remodeling, or building things; being actively involved with her church; gardening; air frying; or just puzzling on one of her hand-built puzzle boards.

Jill was born and raised in St. Marys, Pennsylvania, and has spent the majority of her life in Florida, currently residing in Fort Myers, Florida, where she continues to passionately write full-time regarding success strategies, leadership development, positive mind transformation, critical thinking, and young adult, teen, and adult fiction novels.